by Henry G. Lamond

KILGOUR'S MARE

ILLUSTRATIONS
by Lajos Segner

WILLIAM MORROW AND COMPANY
NEW YORK · 1943

Acknowledgments

This story first appeared in the *Bulletin*, Sydney, in serial form. My thanks are due to the proprietors of the *Bulletin* for their courtesy in granting me the right to republish the story.

My grateful thanks are also due to Mr. E. G. Barrymore ("Cestus" of the *North Queensland Register*), who took a delight in drawing up pedigrees for me, and in discussing horses endlessly; in fact, so great were his enthusiasm and help, that I dedicate this work to him.

H. G. L.

COPYRIGHT - 1943
BY HENRY G. LAMOND

PRINTED IN THE UNITED STATES OF AMERICA

Chapter 1

AWAY IN THE EAST THE SKY WAS LIGHTENING. DOWN among the trees on the creek a magpie hailed the dawn. With a voice flutelike in its richness and purity the bird throbbed the air with great globules of music. A crow called harshly and oared his way heavily on sighing wings. Corellas lifted up their raucous voices, and sported in their morning exercises of aerial gymnastics. A windmill, half-seen on the creek, suddenly woke to life as a wandering puff caught it. Busily, almost as if it was guided by a thinking brain, it swung to face the wind, and its wheel spun with a purr as it set about its day's work.

A day had begun on Meetucka station, on the

Georgina watershed, in the far west of Queensland. It began with the sound of galloping horses. Racing, playing, kicking and bucking as they galloped, the horses were driven to the yard. Cherry, a chestnut mare, reached the gate first. She propped and wheeled. She squealed for the mere joy of living, and she reared and struck blindly to oppose any horse who dared to enter the yard before her. But Cherry's petty resistance was swept aside. The others jostled past her, and in a living stream they poured through the gate. Little spurts of sweat were showing about their flanks and down their shoulders; their manes and tails were dishevelled; their eyes were just a little prominent with excitement, and the red flare of their nostrils showed plainly as they panted.

But they were happy. They were in perfect condition. Their coats shone like burnished metal, and they were fit to face the day.

The horses settled themselves in the yard to make the most of that half-hour spell before the arrival of the men from breakfast. There was an odd little squealing skirmish, a clash of teeth and a shuffling of feet as they paired off, mate with mate, and stood head to tail with one hind-leg resting. Gradually each lower lip hung pendulous, each eye half closed, each head drooped to an easy level, and, unconscious, yet rhythmic, each tail swung to ward the flies from the other's eyes.

Cascade was a stranger. A beautiful eight-year-old chestnut mare, she had not yet any social standing in the mob. She had not reached the position of possessing a mate of her own, of the right to claim one part of the yard as hers, on which she could stand and take her rest, and she was denied the privilege of demanding that another horse should stand head-and-tail with her and swish flies mutually.

She moved tentatively towards Cherry. Cherry lopped her ears, bared her teeth and swung her head as if, like a snake, she was about to strike. Cascade moved away. In her heart she was not afraid of Cherry; but there was an etiquette, and she knew it, about the pairing of horses in the yard. She had not found her footing. Until she was a recognized member she must hover on the outskirts.

Over in one corner old Capsicum was standing alone. Cascade made friendly advances towards her. Capsicum made no response—she did not even deign to open one eye or to lift her head to a higher level. Cascade ranged beside her confidently, and with the comforting feeling that any sort of a mate is better than no mate at all she stood head-and-tail with the old mare and swished flies contentedly.

There was a reason why Capsicum had a corner of the yard to herself and why no others mated with her. That old virago had a temper! Cascade had swished but three times, drawing the plume of her tail lingeringly over the old mare's eyes, when Capsicum demanded better attention. She bared her teeth and chopped sharply at Cascade's buttock. Cascade knew the signal. In horse language that meant "Shake it up! Swing your tail more briskly!" Cascade responded. She increased the pace of her swings and lengthened the radius. Capsicum's face was enveloped in a perfect veil of hair, and not one fly could have found a footing there. Capsicum had no fault to find with that attention. She found fault because there was no fault to find. She struck again with her teeth, and she doubled her body and swung round with her tail twitching in spasmodic jerks.

Cascade knew that signal also. Capsicum had declared war. Her opponent could flee to save herself— she could take the punishment which was to be handed out to her, or she could fight. Cascade was a stranger in a strange yard. Her position had not been determined, and she was not sure where she stood. She elected to escape punishment. She sprang away from Capsicum and fled towards the middle of the yard.

With any of the horses to which she was accustomed that would have sufficed for Capsicum. But this new mare was a stranger. She must be taught her place and a fitting degree of humility. She followed that escaping figure.

As Cascade reached the main body of the horses the lopped ears and twitching tails told her there was no sanctuary there. That old she-fiend Capsicum came charging behind her. Cascade dodged, and, striving to efface herself, slipped into the corner she had left. She cringed there. That was Capsicum's own special corner! In the old mare's bigoted mind that was the height of insolence. She charged. With her mane flying, her eyes glaring, her teeth bare and with her tail streaming behind her, she swept to the attack. She raked Cascade's ribs with tearing teeth and, pressing her in the corner, swung and loosed her thunderbolts of hind hooves.

Cascade cringed and twisted as one broadside took her. As Capsicum was gathering herself for the second she turned. Unflinchingly she took the shock as Capsicum's hooves rattled her ribs; and then her own hooves lifted under Capsicum's belly.

The old mare was surprised. More, she was hurt. In the long run of years her dignity had never suffered such a jolt. It was more than enough. She retired, kicking blindly at nothing when she was well out of range and chopping one inoffensive gelding with raking teeth as she passed him.

Confidently, knowing that her place was won, Cascade looked for a mate beside whom she could stand head-and-tail. She selected Cherry—Cherry, the acknowledged social leader of the yard!—and after a brief introductory nuzzling and smelling of breaths the two mares stood out clear of the others and swished tails in contentment.

"We'd better pension off old Capsicum," Kilgour, the manager of Meetucka, was saying to Harry Peelben as the men came to the yard. "She's a vicious old devil! She might cripple something one of these days. I can't stand these old uns who look for fight for the sake of fighting.

"You're taking the camp out to Galahpootra to-day, aren't you?" he asked. "I'll take this mare out to Mingeri Paddock and put her with Bluff Downs. Tell Paddy to make a fire outside the round yard till we cross-brand her, will you? Hey, Woppida!" he called to a blackboy. "You catch'em that mare Maple belong-it me. No, you fool! Not that one horse Marble. That one Maple—that mare."

A man, he thought, doesn't ride a gelding when he goes among a stallion's mob running bush—not unless he's looking for trouble.

He caught Cascade in the round yard.

"You've been having a fight with something," he muttered, noticing the streak of hair missing from along her ribs.

He bridled the mare, soothed her and petted her while the brands were heating.

"What's amusin' th' boss this mornin', Harry?" one of the men asked. "He's that pleased with himself he'd burst out laughin' if he got a stitch in th' side—he'd reckon it was somethin' ticklin' his ribs."

"He got that chestnut mare from Andy Whelan yesterday," Harry replied abruptly, being economical almost to the point of meanness with speech. "She's got a pedigree as long as your arm."

"Who's goin' to ride her? Billy Brennan, Whelan's horse-tailer, told me that one can go through th' ring of th' bit when she starts buckin' proper."

"She ain't that bad," Harry stated. "Anyway, you needn't spit on your hands, Joe. She's goin' to Bluff Downs."

"H'm-m-m-m," Joe replied judiciously, taking a new view of the mare. "If I was in th' boss's place I'd be whistlin' tunes meself, gettin' a brood mare like that."

Kilgour took the brand from the fire and tested it against a post in the yard. It charred quickly, cleanly, without breaking into flame, and he handed it back to return to the fire. He took off his hat and placed it under the near cheek-strap of the bridle, improvising a one-sided winker, and picked up a stake about three feet long. Then, while Harry held the mare in front, he soothed her and rubbed against her body on the blind side, running his hand down her near thigh.

"She's got the breeder's brand on the near thigh," he mumbled. "The next quarter's the off rib. I hate a rib-brand on a horse. There's room under the breeder's brand. Hand me that brand, Paddy."

Kilgour held the stake in his left hand. He took the brand in his right, pressing the point of the stake against the mare's quarter. That caused her to lean over, tightening the skin, and presenting a drum-tight surface to the brand. With a light touch, firm and quick, he pressed the U9L in one piece against the gleaming skin. For a snap of a second nothing happened. Then, coincident with the swirling plume of smoke and the acrid smell of burnt hair, the mare bounded wildly as the pain stung her.

Harry was crooning unintelligible profanities while he soothed the mare and quietened her. Kilgour threw the brand to Paddy, and snatched the hat from the mare's cheek. He took her muzzle in the crook of his arm, laid his cheek against hers. From deep down in his throat a steady rumble sounded while words poured from his lips—words which had no place in any modern lexicon, which were meaningless, profane, blasphemous and yet which the mare seemed to understand as a message of peace.

The men caught their horses and saddled them. Those needed for the camp were drafted out in a separate yard. Kilgour, riding Maple and leading Cascade running beside him, started for Mingeri.

It was late in March. The season had been good and the grass, mellow and rich, waved before the wind. Summer was abating slightly. Already giant puffs from the south-east heralded the steady trade winds which were to take possession of the land for the next six to nine months.

Birds of many varieties, having reared their first clutch of chickens for the year, were congregating in big flocks, filling the air with their cries and feasting on the bounteous provender of the earth. The smaller creeks had ceased running, but all the holes were full, and along the banks trees drooped under heavy foliage. In short, the earth was responding to the rains—full, replete and bursting with life. And the flies were everywhere—sickly, nauseating, clinging.

Kilgour rode up along Mingeri Creek. He headed for the big claypan flat above Camp Oven Hole, swinging easily to the action of his horse. When he lifted his hat to scratch his head, or to let the wind play on it, his hair showed grizzled and streaked with grey. He looked just what he knew himself to be—a plain bushman and stock-lover, suntanned, lean, wiry, with wrinkles showing about his eyes.

He knew the stallion and mares would be where he found them on the claypan, walking in a ring, so that the earth broke up like fine flour, keeping the flies off them. There were between twenty and thirty mares. On the outskirts were ten or a dozen with foals, spindly-shanked little strangers which hugged their mothers' flanks in fear and wonder of the world. A blazing chestnut, every inch a stallion, showed prominently, even though all the horses were at rest. They were dozing, lifting an occasional hoof and setting it down again, swinging tails incessantly.

Suddenly one of the mares sensed a stranger's approach. She did not move or utter a sound, yet the warning spread from her over the mob. Instantly all heads were erect; ears pricked. The mob was alert.

Only one horse called. Full and rich, the stallion's clarion challenge rang through the air. Bluff Downs breasted his way through his brood, pushing mares aside. He came out to meet that which approached him.

The stallion stood clear of the mob and challenged again. He snorted stertorously, then he raked dust, threw billowing clouds of earth in the air behind him.

Kilgour dismounted and dropped Maple's reins on the ground. Holding Cascade's halter, he advanced a little to meet the horse.

Bluff Downs swung round the led mare and swooped in on Maple. He whinnied to her as he came, and with a rush he surged up beside her, nuzzling her nostrils with his.

Maple squealed her protest, lopped her ears and struck blindly. The rebuff satisfied him. He left her and came towards Kilgour and Cascade.

Kilgour, knowing the fight that would have been on hand had he been fool enough to ride a gelding, admired the superb masculinity of the horse.

Bluff Downs reached Cascade. Whinnying softly, he advanced his nostrils to those of the mare. He slipped along her side and sniffed behind her shoulder. Then his whinnyings took a new note.

Cascade resented those abrupt advances. She squealed, switched her tail and kicked.

The stallion bounded back. Posturing superbly, his tail arched, the wind ruffling the mane on his crest as he bowed his head, he advanced again.

Kilgour let the mare go. Undecided, she hesitated whether to trot back to Maple or to go to the brood mares ahead of her.

Bluff Downs lowered his head, lopped his ears, swept in behind the mare, chopped her on the buttocks with his teeth. When she bounded and tried to swing back he headed her off. He propped and wheeled her when she attempted to dodge, and, close behind her, with his head held high to avoid the retaliatory kicks, he shepherded her into his mob and merged her with them. He followed her among them, reared, squealed, raked dust, curvetted—he impressed her with his might and he fascinated her with his beauty.

The brood was disturbed. Some of the outside members spread and nibbled at the short pickings of grass on the flat. Bluff Downs left Cascade. For the time being the new member of his brood could wait. He burst through the mob, lowered his head and swung it with a snake-like action. He lopped his ears, showed the whites of his eyes and bared his teeth. Then, in a fury, he swept round the mob. Those mares knew the rules, the implacable spirit of their lord. They scuttled back to the ring. One mare on the outskirts hesitated. She was a light bay with a chestnut colt at foot. Palpably she was nervous, and undecided whether to flee or to return to the mob, she cringed in fear and shrunk in on herself as the stallion approached her. Then, when he was almost upon her she fled in terror, galloping blindly.

Bluff Downs raced beside her, chopping at her, and with each bite raising small tufts of hair which floated in the wind. He chased her a hundred yards or more from the mob. He raced in front of her and stopped her in her tracks. He wheeled her back and chivvied her in another direction. When she sought to regain the safety of the mob he intercepted her and drove her out on the flat. He would not let her enter the mob. He would not let her race away. The mare was wet with the sweat of terror. A flabby thing in her fear, she rolled in her stride.

"That's Susette," Kilgour muttered, talking to himself. "I knew the horse disliked her, but I didn't think he hated her that badly."

Suddenly Bluff Downs reared slightly, curvetted and uttered a peculiar little gurgling whinny.

Susette came to him. She came falteringly, unwillingly, seemingly in a mesmeric trance and unable to control herself. She came, each slow step singly, and a dozen times she hesitated. But she came as though tied to a string, slowly and surely.

Bluff Downs curvetted, rearing and swinging on his hind-legs.

The mare came to him, sweating fear as she advanced. She drew nearer, balanced on the hair-trigger of flight, and at last she was close enough to meet the outstretched nostrils of the horse.

"What can you expect of the progeny of such a mating?" Kilgour asked himself, mounting Maple to ride home. "I'll lay the odds to thrippence that it ain't a horse."

Chapter 2

HALF-WAY THROUGH APRIL THE TOWNSHIP OF Iladda, the centre and gathering point of that district, decided to hold a race-meeting. Programmes were printed and sent to the various stations. Kilgour, going out to the camp to note how the branding was progressing, took one with him.

"Here you are, Harry," he advised his head stockman. "The township's holding a meeting on the twenty-fourth of May. It's a grassfed affair for station horses. What about it?"

"What's it in aid of?" Harry wanted to know.

"This don't make a pretence of being in aid of anything," Kilgour said. "Might be a publican's benefit. Any horses you'd like to send?"

"Them Bluffs is too green yet," Harry said. "They're only three, an' th' first of 'em is only broke a few months. I'd like to meet 'em next year, an' th' year after, with some of them colts. Still, we can hold our end up with th' ol' horses. There's Jujube, an' Swallow, an' Glacier, an' Heiress, an' Zoe, an' one or two others."

Harry was inclined to loquacity on one subject only: horses and racing. That was a long speech, for him.

"I think we'll give it a flick," the manager observed. "Of course, it's a tea-and-sugar bushranger's meeting. We can't win much, though we can lose a dickens of a lot if we ain't careful. Anyway, it does the men good."

"I'll take Wraith, too," Harry decided. "She's pretty slippy for a bit, an' with th' work she's been doin', an' th' solid feed of this time of th' year, she'll run her five furlongs. You don't know what other horses is comin', I suppose?"

"I haven't the faintest idea," Kilgour admitted. "It's pretty much of a certainty, though, that Evans is going to bring Linen Duster. That mare must be fifteen if she's a day. It's blasted murder. He's racing the guts out of her."

"She won th' Handicap at th' last 'Burra meetin'."

"What if she did? What's it matter if she did win a thirty-quid trophy an' a few bits of bets? That mare's done her day—she did it before Evans got her. She might have thrown something fit to take her place as a horse. You can't breed good stuff from the frame of a wreck, Harry."

"Suppose not," Harry agreed. "I hear he's got some good youngsters by that new horse of his, Lapidist."

"He might have, Harry. Lapidist is by Grafton. What chance d'you think a Galopin horse has of getting good stock-horses? That blood's too fiery. It's too excitable. I doubt if it'll stand punishment. I mean the long work and slugging. That Galopin stuff fizzes like soda-water. There are exceptions, of course. But, if Evans gets racing his two-year-old stuff, he's riding for a fall."

"Th' meetin's on th' twenty-fourth of May," Harry read the poster. "I'll have them horses ready by then. I suppose you'll be runnin' Nebo for yourself, will you?"

Harry continued his work. The horses for the meeting had sufficient rough training to allow them to gallop in public. The Meetucka party, with their horses, their camp-followers and retinue reached Iladda on the eve of the races.

Iladda, in common with all western townships, consisted of a pub, a police-station, a post office, a herd of goats, a litter of empty bottles and battered kerosene tins, and a collection of corrugated-iron buildings which were known as houses. For the greater part of the year it drowsed, with only an occasional drunk to give it life. At race-meetings it bloomed a while.

Kilgour, watching the coatless men coming and going to and from the bar, was approached by Evans.

"Hullo, Evans," he said. "How goes it? I see by the nominations you've brought a string of horses. Old Linen Duster's top-weight for the Handicap: eleven-ten. It's a big weight for a grassfed horse over a mile."

"She is grassfed, like all the rest of them," Evans

answered quickly, scenting an implication that his mare had been fed secretly. "She's not too old—she'll be twelve on the first of August. I'm thinking of putting her to the stud before she breaks down. She ought to give Bluff Downs a chance he rarely gets—mating with a mare of that quality. I brought another two-year-old filly. By Lapidist from Seething—stud-book stuff. She crippled herself, unfortunately. I don't mind swapping you a couple of services. I'll send these two mares to Bluff Downs, and allow you to send two of yours to Lapidist. How about it?"

"Oh, very well," Kilgour replied gruffly. He felt irritable, but added: "We'll wet it. What's yours?"

At the course races were run and other business was conducted—between drinks. The betting opened and became freer, coincident and proportionately with the increase to the pile of empty bottles behind the booth.

Bluff Tom Hopkins, sterling fellow and manager of Parrapituri Downs, collected a group of brother-managers.

"These publicans' benefits are right enough," he concluded. "But we want a decent club. How about us getting together and forming a club of our own?"

"Good egg!" Kilgour agreed. "I've been thinking the same thing, Tom. Exclusive, strict, straight—will that do for a slogan?"

The voice of the race-meeting secretary interrupted them.

"Weigh out for th' Publicans' Handicap!" the secretary called, ringing a bell with one hand and wiping his mouth with the back of the other as he moved away from the bar. "Weigh out for th' Publicans' Handicap."

"Even money th' field!" the bookmakers took up their chorus. "Evens th' Duster. Two to one Flagpole. Three to one Nebo. Two to one bar one. Here, four to one Bezique an' Straddler. Three to one bar one! I'll lay! I'll lay! I'll lay! Even money Linen Duster. Six to one Styx. Who wants to back one?"

The field went to the post. Linen Duster, though as well known as the township itself, received curious and admiring attention. A bay mare, low and long, she moved cleanly, and her eyes showed full, lustrous and intelligent. But there was an indefinable something about her which prompted Kilgour to screw his own eyes in a maze of wrinkles while he watched her. The mare's eyes may have been just a shade too prominent, the lustre which shone from them perhaps a trifle glazed. Patches of sweat showed about her flanks and down the slope of her shoulders. As she was going to the post her tail twitched nervously, half swung in a semi-circle, then jerked from side to side.

"Poor little mare," Kilgour muttered under his breath. "I knew it was coming. It's come!"

"Go!" the starter shouted, swinging his red flag to the ground.

A dozen horses bounded forward in a swirl of dust. In a scramble and rush they jostled to the first turn. There they strung out slightly, and Styx played merrily in the lead. A couple of horses showed clear of the ruck near him, and then in a bunch they straggled away again to a dwindling tail. They raced along the back, seeming to move like mechanical toys in the distance. Styx had dropped from the lead and was lost to sight. Design ripped along in front, lengths clear. Just ahead of the ruck Linen Duster's, Flagpole's and Nebo's colours could be picked out. Away out behind, toiling hopelessly, Brusque followed the pack.

With a ribbon of dust following behind, with the clatter of galloping hooves and the shimmer of bright silk, they turned into the running. Linen Duster's yellow jacket with black spots showed prominently. Behind it a blurred kaleidoscope of jumbled colours mingled together. The mare was racing strongly—though to the trained eye she may have appeared to be labouring slightly—and already the crowd was acclaiming her victory.

"Linen Duster!" one solitary voice roared. "Li'n Duster!" the chorus echoed. "Come on, Li'n Duster! Li'n Duster! Hooray!"

Suddenly the mare faltered. She lost the machine-like precision of her action. She floundered. She rolled and wallowed. She climbed in her stride, and the rushing phalanx from behind swallowed her, engulfed her and hid her.

The race was run and won. The judge made his declaration, and the clerk of the scales testified to the correct weight.

"I'll pay Nebo," the bookmakers shouted. "I'll pay Nebo. Pay Nebo. Bet on th' next. Even money Malcolm. Three to one bar one. I'll pay!"

Linen Duster, tied to a tree, was standing with her legs wide-braced. She hung her head low, and her tail, half-raised, was flying a signal of her distress. She quivered and trembled, and gulped great gallons of air. She was too spent to show any excitement and too exhausted to open her eyes or lift her head.

"She was short of a gallop," Evans confided to Kilgour as they stood out from the mare looking at her.

"I told Ted she was short. You saw the way she went to pieces, did you? She choked. Too fat inside. I would have liked her to win her last race. In fact, I backed her to win. Still she'll breed a great foal to Bluff Downs."

"Do you want me to put her to the horse immediately?" Kilgour asked, anything but pleased about it.

"If you would—she and Sethia. You'll take them down with you, will you?"

The races went on.

Back at the station Kilgour instructed his head stockman. "Take these two mares out and let 'em go with Bluff Downs. Take care of the old mare, Harry—she deserves a better fate than any we can give her. And, Harry, I want you to have a look at Cascade when you're out there. See all's well with her."

Chapter 3

THE STORMS CAME EARLY IN JANUARY. ALMOST OVERnight, the khaki earth took a new coat. Tender little shoots of green sprang into being and a mantle of verdure covered the ground.

Further storms followed. The horses huddled miserably, tails to the driving rain, and with water running over their quarters and dribbling down their hocks. Then the wet season commenced in earnest. Mere pads and tracks became rivulets. Gullies tore and rushed with spume-strewn waters. Creeks roared in their might, and the sodden ground squelched water at every hoof-track.

With the rains the flies came in countless millions. Those stinging serpents of the air, the sandflies, made all animal life a constant torture.

It was a good season, and all Nature responded—full measure, pressed down and brimming over.

Strangely enough, coincident with the rains, a sudden drop of foals occurred in the brood. When the drenched earth dried itself, shaking its mane of grass and laughing in the sun, ten little strangers ranged beside their mothers and mingled with the mob. Flyrings were reopened and worked to the full. But even that did not afford perfect protection from the sandflies. The mares were constantly on the move during the ten days after the last rain, which was the period of the sandflies' life.

While crossing a washed-out creek Sheba's month-old foal, playing carelessly, blundered into the wet silt. It floundered, struggled desperately. But there was no firm footing beneath its hooves, and gradually it sank until it was mid-rib deep.

The rest of the mares trotted on, ever striving to get away from the sandflies. Sheba returned to her foal. She hovered on the brink, neighing piteously and with her head outstretched towards the foal wallowing in the mud. Feeling her way tentatively, she waded in to where the foal was stuck, and there nuzzled it, crooning to it and licking the clinging mud from it.

Bluff Downs suddenly discovered one of his mares had deserted the brood. He raced to the lead of the mob, swung them abruptly and brought them back to the bank of the creek on which Sheba had climbed and was standing while she watched the foal. Without pause, and with his low-held head swaying in snake-like undulations, he charged the mare. He swung between her and her foal, and with a chop sent her scurrying back to the brood.

Sheba called once. From the bed of the creek a piteous whinny replied to her, and she turned and raced back to the gully.

The stallion followed her. He swept in between her and the bank of the creek and tried to drive her back to the waiting brood.

Sheba squealed, reared and struck blindly. She snapped with her teeth and swung to lash with her heels. Berserk in anger, bold beyond belief through fear for her foal, a fiend in her fury, she swept the horse aside. She raced to the brink of the bank, plunged into the silt and stood beside her helpless foal. She was quivering, distraught. But she dared the horse!

Bluff Downs followed. He lifted hair from her rump with his chopping bites. He shouldered her over, and by main force pushed her up the bank. When she reared and struck at him he reached across and took her by the nape of the neck, his strong teeth closing as a vice and making the mare wince and cringe in on herself. He swung her in front of him, bashed her with his striking hooves. Then, all opposition quelled, he drove her to the brood.

It was night when a sound caused the foal to prick its ears, to whinny softly and struggle to escape.

Sheba had returned. She stood beside her foal. She nuzzled it. Deep down in her throat she crooned to it. In her helplessness she walked about it, and a dozen times climbed the bank, stood on top on the firm ground and called to the foal to follow her. Had she been a story-book mare she would have taken it in her teeth and lifted it clear of the bog. But she was only bush-bred, one of a brood, and though her love was as strong and passionate as any mythical heroine she could not do impossibilities.

Four o'clock the following afternoon she was still there, unwittingly, by her trampling, securing it against any prospect of escape. Warned by an inexplicable and unanalysed sense, she lifted her head. On the bank two red dingoes looked down on the stricken foal and licked their chops.

Like a flash the mare charged, squealing her anger. She spun on a pin's-head space as she pursued a dodging dingo; her teeth snapped a bare hair's-breadth from the back of the dog as it swung round the trunk of a tree. She smashed at it with her battering forefeet. She reared; then, twisting and doubling, turning and wheeling, she drove the dingoes over the edge of the plain and lost them in the scrub.

Sweat lathered her sides and dripped to the ground. She struggled for breath; the wide flare of her nostrils heaved red. She lifted her head high, snorted her anger and her challenge. Then she started to trot back the couple of miles to where she had left her foal.

Midway Bluff Downs met her. Her resistance was futile. The stallion merged her with the brood again, and with almost devilish cunning kept beside her. Yet, after a dozen attempts, Sheba sneaked out of one side of the mob and galloped wildly. As she propped on the bank of the creek two red figures slunk away from the remains of what had been a foal. The air was heavy with the scent of blood. Through it drifted a faint tinge of the odour of dingoes.

About the end of March Cascade left the brood on her secret mission. She had selected a clump of gidgee-trees out on the downs below Pigeon Bend. She went there. Just as the sun was setting she nickered softly and lowered her head to lick a wet bundle of life which lay on the ground before her. Crooning incessantly, mumbling softly, talking in her own language, she ignored her pain in the happiness which had come to her.

A chestnut filly, marked similarly to its mother, staggered to its feet and stood swaying on tottering legs. It took a stride forward, tripping uncertainly, and then its little pink tongue slobbered its mother's chest between her front legs.

Cascade was uneasy. Perhaps she was slightly embarrassed. She nuzzled the thing with her nostrils, and in raking slabs which shook the foal's frail body all over she licked it from end to end. She pushed it away from her chest gently; took a long stride forward and brought its nostrils level with her flank.

The little thing nuzzled with renewed energy. It slobbered lustily, and when its head was hidden under its mother's flank it staggered on its weak legs from the energy of ecstasy. Its absurd wisp of a tail was held horizontally, and it bumped vigorously and slobbered and gulped in its contentment.

Cascade stood with one hind-leg eased, exposing her udder to the foal. But the wonder of it all could not

AMATHEA					
	BLUFF DOWNS 18 Ch.	ST HIPPO 27 B.	ST LEGER 3 B.	DONCASTER 5	STOCKWELL 3
					MARIGOLD 5
				ATLANTIS	THORMANBY 4
					HURRICANE 3
			HIPPONA	ROBINSON CRUSOE 13	ANGLER 2
					CHRYSOLITE 13
				LAMORNA	FIREWORKS 10
					NIGHTLIGHT (Imp.) 27
		HILLGROVE Ch.	VIGOR 12 Ch.	CHEVIOT (Imp.) 2	ADVENTURER 12
					GREY STOCKING 2
				VIRGO	THE DRUMMER 1
					BRITANNIA 12
			NATAL DOWNS Br.	DARABBA 17	REUGNEY 5
					MATCHLESS 17
				MARYVALE	CONFUCIUS 13
					FILAGO 18
	ASCADE Ch.	FAIRLIGHT Br.	THE HERMIT 29 Br.	ROBINSON CRUSOE 13	ANGLER 2
					CHRYSOLITE 13
				PILGRIMAGE	KELPIE 1
					YOUNG EMILY 29
			MOUNT EMU Br.	LORD MARIAN 13 Bay	ORMONDE 4
					MAID MARIAN 13
				LYNDHURST	ADONIS 39
					MABLE *
		DODONA Ch.	DOTSWOOD Br.	THE DOGE 2 Brown	GOLDSBROUGH 13
					VENETIA 2
				BURDEKIN	COLLECTOR 5
					MEDUSA †
			MINERVA Ch.	EMIGRANT 4 Bay	LAUREATE 5
					EMUTE 4
				MEDUSA Ch.	CONFUCIUS 13
					MEDINA ‡ Grey

† Confucius—Medina.

* Old Australian unnumbered family.
‡ By Snowden from a mare by Haley's Arab, said to be a thoroughbred.

let her rest quietly. A dozen times she turned to caress, and the foal had to regain the udder. And all the time Cascade talked to it, crooning, mumbling, whispering and gurgling softly.

The foal drank and drank—drank until its wee paunch swelled, and it braced itself wide to support itself. Then it turned round once, bent at the knees and hocks, and with a grunt dropped to the ground. It stretched itself out straight, and almost on the instant its eyes shut and it slept.

For five hours Cascade never stirred save to switch her tail incessantly and occasionally to lower her head to smell the sleeping youngster on the ground. The sky in the east was reddening when she lowered her head again. This time her nostrils lightly brushed the foal behind the wither.

Ten thousand times ten thousand generations had taught the foal the meaning of that signal. Instantly it struggled to its feet, alert and with its ears pricked. Then, with all the confidence imaginable, it went to its mother's flank again.

This time the novelty of the position had worn from Cascade. She let the foal drink quietly, standing in a manner to give it the greatest ease. But when the foal was little more than what it might have considered half-way through its meal Cascade moved forward.

With a long, lingering and drawing squeeze the foal let its mother's teat slide through its lips. Instinct may have taught it the inflexible rule: The only full drink allowed is that immediately following birth; after that all drinks are cut short by the mother. It is a simple rule, and beautiful in its simplicity: A full drink brings on a feeling of contentment and a desire to sleep which is not suitable to the mare who may wish to wander; a half-drink leaves the foal with the desire for more and with the inclination to follow the source of the supply—its mother.

Cascade walked out on the downs and headed for the fly-ring above Camp Oven. She knew she would find the brood there. The little thing stepped bravely, its head held jauntily; its small mane rippled in the wind, its legs planted uncertainly. Its short tail, the hair still crimped in waves, was arched. It looked with wonder about it, and seemed to take an interest in what it saw. But, be it fear or caution, it hugged its mother's side, and that comforting touch was against it all the time.

A few hundred yards from the brood, and even as Bluff Downs was sounding his neighing call of challenge and welcome, Cascade stopped short. A man was riding across the downs towards her! With the inherent fear which all young mothers feel for their first young prompting her, she turned from the brood and raced towards the creek.

The foal's long legs were seemingly tangled in complicated knots, and it appeared to have difficulty in retaining its balance. But it kept beside its galloping mother. More, by some weird sense it kept on the opposite side of its mother, keeping her all the time between it and the unknown danger.

Like a streak of flame in his action, Bluff Downs left the mob. He gathered in the flying mare, swung her, and in one stride he had her wheeled and racing towards the brood. He merged her with them while he raced round to steady some mares which were inclined to run away. Then he stood out clear to look at the horseman who was riding past.

At the head station Harry knocked at the door of the manager's office.

"I come by th' brood in Mingeri this mornin'," he announced.

"Eh?" Kilgour asked. "See Cascade? She must be near foaling."

"A chestnut filly born last night, I think."

"What's it like?"

"Same markin's as its mother. Strong. Big bones an' joints."

Harry reported on the brood. When he had gone Kilgour took Cascade's pedigree down from its nail on the wall. He considered it, talking of her breeding to himself. After a long soliloquy he added the name of Cascade's foal. He called it Amathea.

Chapter 4

WHEN CASCADE TOOK HER PLACE IN THE BROOD Bluff Downs followed her among the mares. He played about her, curvetting and squealing his pleasure. Then, the first wild outburst of joy having passed, he took station on the outside of the ring and stood head-and-tail with old Clara.

Cascade was nervous. This was her first foal. It was the most wonderful thing in the wide world. She was fearful for it, and sooner than stand head-and-tail in comfort with any other obliging mate she preferred the discomfort of the flies so that she could stand out clear and attend to her baby. She started in alarm every time it moved. Every minute she nuzzled it anxiously, and she crooned to it incessantly.

Other foals came to have a look at it—the matrons

were so used to youngsters that the novelty had long since passed into monotony. When strangers approached it the little thing spread its legs wide, jammed its tail tight, lopped its ears, rolled the whites of its eyes, and with bared teeth commenced a jerky clock-work champing with its jaws. It was all very fearsome and inspiring, perhaps; but at the same time it was just a little ludicrous. Still, it was the Law! All foals did it, and continued to do it, up to an age of eight to ten months.

Exactly like a new child at a strange school, that little foal had to find its footing. One day passed—two—three—and in a week it was absorbed as part of the play-team of foals. It made its own particular mates and friends; it had its dislikes and peculiar aversions; it took part in mock fights and put its whole heart into the games which were played. Its mother was its protector, its guardian, its food-supply and its adoring slave.

Repetition never seemed to stale the variety or to drain the depths of that wonderful affection! Old Babette had mothered ten foals—six by the previous stallion and four by Bluff Downs. She rejoined the brood with her fifth Bluff Downs foal—a tottery-legged little chestnut—staggering at her side. That old mare saw all the wonder of heaven in that new foal. She guarded it as solicitously, as earnestly, and the love-croonings of her soft whinnyings were as constant as any mare with first progeny. The past was forgotten, and all the wonders of the previous foals were lost in the joy and perfection of the present. Truly, when seasonal conditions are good, the lot of a young foal is much to be envied.

Early in April the first tinge of winter came. The flies abated noticeably, and with the grass still carrying a streak of green, and at its highest state of nutritious content, the brood literally lolled in comfort and ease. They were sleek, shining, strong and in great heart. The foals were commencing to nibble daintily at short pickings, and the fullness of their mothers' udders was a supply which never ran short. They played. They raced. They bucked and skipped and fought.

They followed their mothers to water. Prompted by curiosity, the little things sniffed that strange fluid which lapped their fetlocks, and which their mothers swallowed so eagerly. Then derisive little nostrils were curled while the little head was held high, and almost it seemed those cocksure youngsters laughed in silence at the thought of drinking such insipid stuff while full udders of mellow milk were theirs for the taking. Life was good.

It was good to roll in the soft dust on the claypan above Camp Oven. It was good to wriggle in ecstatic pleasure and to paw the air with dainty hooves while the hot grains of fine earth tickled the skin. Particularly was it good to gather together in the faint light of early dawn, when all was fresh and crisp, and to race endlessly over the dewless grass while panting mothers laboured behind in an effort to catch up—calling, all the time calling, to wayward youngsters to return and behave properly. There were a dozen things every day which required investigation. The foals would gather in curious circles, delicate nostrils extended. They would walk warily and take fright, scampering in mad delight from a bogus terror, or they would return sedately to their mothers' sides, the mystery solved. All life was good.

Late in May they were mustered for branding. This was a ticklish operation. Bluff Downs was an intolerant lord of his harem who had to be humoured. The foals themselves were living crackers enclosed in soap bubbles. The mares were on the tenterhooks of anxiety. All required their own special handling, each method differing from the other, and the whole had to be combined and handled as one unit.

Kilgour, a natural horse-lover, shook his shoulders and shed his office worries. He went out with the men to muster the brood. Mustering them was easy—the stallion kept them all in one mob and there were no stragglers to hunt and find. Handling them was a different matter.

"I'll steady the lead, Harry," Kilgour called, wheeling his mount and riding in front of the driven horses to prevent them racing. "Look out for old Bluff. Sometimes he don't like a man riding ahead."

The mob jogged along, Kilgour riding in the lead and steadying them. A dozen times Bluff Downs came out, his neck arched, snorting and pawing the ground, to have a closer look at the man in the lead, perhaps to usurp that privilege, and, generally, to demonstrate to the mares that, though in bondage, he was still the lord of the mob. The man in the lead dared not pay too much attention to the horse lest he give that animal a false idea of his position—few animals can detect fear in a man quicker than a horse, particularly a stallion. At the same time, Kilgour had to be alert, his eyes looking behind, as it were, in case of a sudden rush.

"Hairt, th' horse! Steady, th' old stallion! Whoa, th' mares!"

Odd fools of foals caused a little trouble at the gates. They raced blindly along the fence, unable to see the opening through which the mob had passed. That threw the brood into disorder. Other foals caught the infection. Old mares, just settling down nicely and accepting the inevitable, were sure their individual foals were being killed. They whinnied and galloped aimlessly.

It was the stallion who restored order. He swept those mares together, checked others which were inclined to break. He steadied the whole mob, stood there, arrogant, defiant, picturesque with the wind playing through his mane and spraying his tail, and he declined to allow them to move until they calmed. It was the instinct of his sex and breed asserting itself.

The mob was yarded and left there the night to steady off and cool down. Next morning Kilgour perched himself on the top rail of the pound yard as the branders came through with their dams. On his knees he balanced a book, and in it he made note of foals and descriptions.

"Bay filly. Faint running star. Near hind stocking and off hind heel white. By Bluff Downs from Pattie.

Branded U9L over 138 near shoulder. Foaled November, last year. Good egg! Let 'em through into the round yard, there. One, three, eight is the number, Harry—one, three, eight."

In the round yard old Pattie edged about the rails carefully. She was not excited—she had been there before. Harry, standing in the middle of the yard, with a head-rope coiled in his hand, worked things until he had the foal running nearly abreast with the mare, though slightly ahead of her, and on the outside. With a hissing sigh a loop flew through the air, hung for a space while hovering over the mare's wither, and dropped over the foal's head and round its neck on the other side of the mare.

"Pull head-rope," he snapped. "Don't open that gate to let th' old mare out, Mick, till we get th' foal more'n half across th' yard."

As the loop fell on it, and was snapped tight, the foal gave a wild leap, landing stiff-legged six feet out in front of its mother. It gave another wriggle and a twist, sprayed a shower of dust, and with a squeal it left the ground again. This time it chafed its mother's chest with the rope. She caught the excitement and, flabby old fool that she was, she also commenced to career madly. The foal spun like a Catherine-wheel. It screamed its fear and yelled its rage. But each time it plunged, and every time it gave any slack on the rope, it was dragged a few more feet towards the branding post.

"Open that gate, Mick, an' let th' ol' mare out."

Pattie ran out, glad to get away from the terror of

the yard. Her old flanks flapped, and she whinnied to her foal. She ranged up and down outside the rails in an effort to get back to the yard which she had left and where her baby was undergoing the torments.

The foal was panting in whistling gasps, its head held forward on its stretched neck, and its forefeet propped in front. It swayed as it stood, and already spurts of sweat were breaking out on it.

"Get in on the thing," Kilgour called. "Blast it, man! Don't get playing quoits with it! Get right in on it. A choking foal won't kick. That's the style."

Joe slipped in, leant against the foal, and by his own weight cast the thing off its balance.

The work went on.

Kilgour kept an even and disinterested voice, in spite of a feeling of pride when he took the description: "Chestnut filly, clean-cut crooked stripe on face, two fore and near hind feet white, by Bluff Downs from Cascade. U9L over 146 near shoulder. Foaled during March."

"One white leg, buy a horse; two white legs, try a horse; three white legs—" one of the men commenced to chant the old quatrain.

"Three white legs, look about him," Kilgour interpolated. "Very well, look about her. She ain't three months old yet. She'll invite inspection. She's right.

"I don't think we'll rope this thing, Harry," he added. "She might hurt herself. I used to be able to throw 'em without ropes. I think I can still do it. Catch Cascade and put a bridle on her."

The mare was bridled. She was led out of the yard.

Kilgour, standing near the gate, crowded the foal over as it tried to follow its mother. Then things happened in a hurry. Cascade reared, struck, and tried to get back to her foal. She was snapped out and the gate was slammed in her face. Kilgour leapt and threw his right arm over the foal's neck, just in front of the wither. He swung his hip round under her neck, and with his legs propped out in front he checked her plunges. Swinging, he swept her muzzle over the crook of his right arm, and, pressing down on her neck with his right hand, he lifted her muzzle and turned slowly to the left.

The foal stumbled, recovered, tried to fight, and sank on its buttocks—that paralysing weight on its spinal column, just in front of the wither, numbing it. The man rolled it over on its side, holding its head twisted up, and Harry dropped on its flank and whipped its tail through its hind-legs. The foal squealed and tried to fight. But it was helpless—its master nerves were held as in a vice, and it had to submit. And not one hair of its small body had been displaced, its skin was not scratched, and it had not sprung a sweat!

On his perch on the top rail Kilgour filled in the description of the newly-branded foal. He smiled to himself, and in the column reserved for the name he wrote: "Amathea (Amie)."

Chapter 5

FATTER SINGH HOBBLED HIS CAMELS AND LEFT THEM while he prepared his stall at the course in readiness for the races next day. He was barely out of sight when a big old bull stretched himself, lurched to his feet, and with the last heave of his widespread front legs snapped a rotten hobble-strap above his knees.

The bull shambled away from the mob into the coolibah-trees along the river-banks, wandering aimlessly. He sought satisfaction. He did not really know what it was he wished to satisfy. He only knew he wanted company and loathed it at the same time. He wanted to travel, and found no pleasure in travelling. Food made no appeal to him, and he stalked blindly through scrubs of the most tempting gidgee-trees—that ambrosia of the camel world. He was discontented, dissatisfied. He was prepared to fight.

Late in the afternoon he heard the music of bells ahead of him, out from Corella Hole. He ambled on eagerly. To him, in country where camels carry bells, it seemed to have meaning.

As he burst through a fringe of trees he came on a team feeding on an open flat. It belonged to Red Dick, the big-gun carrier.

Some of those horses were used to camels. They paid no attention other than to draw a little closer together and to keep an eye on the wanderer. But Rory was no ordinary horse, as any one could hear when Rory's owner was feeling the effects of the publican's efforts on his behalf.

"I'm th' gun carrier on th' roads," Red Dick would announce vaingloriously. "I've got th' best team, an' me stallion's th' king of th' track. Where I camps all th' other carriers has to make way for me. Rory, me stallion, can beat any other horse on th' roads. Rory's a stallion! He ain't none of yer make-weight rubbish. Rory takes a twenty-four inch collar. An' he fills it, too! When Rory gets down to it an' heaves he makes th' chains crack an' ring again. I've got th' best draught stallion on th' roads—a real draught stallion —an' when Rory gets out on th' walk-about other stallions has got to make way for him or get chewed up! Fill 'em up. Here's to Rory, th' king of th' roads!"

Still it was no shame to Rory that, when that ghastly apparition bore down on him—that fearsome wonder from an unknown world which carried an abominable scent pregnant with terror—he swung and blundered after a mare which suddenly bolted.

Rory galloped, rolling in his stride, his great bunches of muscles cording and springing and his giant hooves striking rolling thunder from the ground beneath him. He stopped once, his sides wet with sweat, his breath coming in great gulps and his flanks heaving. He swung about, his head high and the wind playing through his mane. Then his nerve broke again, and he continued his headlong flight.

The camel continued his aimless wanderings. He had long lost the reverberations of Rory's hoof-beats.

Rory blundered on, stopping occasionally to listen and again turning and continuing his flight. He had dropped his mad gallop and trotted. He did not know where he was going. His nerves were shaken; he had lost his reason for the time being. His one desire was to get away from the horror of the camel.

Night came. Suddenly Rory faltered, tripped, sprawled forward and recovered himself. There was a twanging of wires and jangle of strands. He had fallen over a fence in the darkness, sustaining no hurt other than a little hair chafed from above the knees.

Rory was moved to a fresh burst of terror, but he collected himself, swung about on his hind-legs, turned to face what might be following him. Across the night he sent his stertorous snort of challenge.

The nameless terror had left him. He was a horse once more. He held his head high, his ears pricked, his eyes blazed. He looked his part.

Gradually a soothing spirit took Rory. There was a reassuring scent of horses in the air. The pads of their travelling were on the ground before him.

Rory lowered his head and commenced to crop the grass. He sought the tracks of other horses, and, in the manner of his sex and kind, covered them with his scent. He fed contentedly along the pad, following it to water. He reached the water and drank peacefully. He came out on the bank of the hole and rolled in the dust. Then, perfectly at ease, he picked up the tracks again and followed them out to where his senses told him the mob would be gathered. It was early spring, with a good season and rich food, and Rory's blood was running red and hot in his veins. He wanted company. He wanted more than company—he desired mates.

Just as the sun was rising, and even as the morning breeze was ruffling the leaves of the trees, Rory came out on the plain above Camp Oven Hole. About thirty horses were gathered there, and Rory's instinct, or his sense of smell, told him that most of them, if not all, were mares. He swung round a little clump of gidgee and stood clear.

Rory was a glorious sample of his breed. He was a rich bay with black points, his face blazed with the Clydesdale mark. He was big without being huge; heavy without being massive; tremendously powerful without loss of activity. His muscles drew up in great bunches and swelled under his skin, and when he arched his neck and bowed his head living waves rippled along his shoulders and crest.

He pawed the ground once, then neighed to the mares.

From the centre of the group of mares a horse clothed in flame forced his way through. Bluff Downs held his head high and arched his tail. He raked billows of dust, and clarion-clear in its challenge his ringing neigh echoed over the plain. The wind rippled his mane and sprayed his tail; the rising sun bathed his chestnut coat in flashes of fire.

Rory advanced twenty yards. He lifted each big hoof and placed it carefully with a stilty action as he held his great muscles drawn for immediate use.

Bluff Downs stepped out to meet him; stepped daintily, mincingly, the muscles of his crest corded and bunched in great knots.

The stallions faced each other, standing not more than thirty feet apart. Rory was a battle-scarred warrior who knew all the rules of war and all the tricks of a scrap. Further, he was panting with desire and swollen with the urge of conquest. Bluff Downs had never fought another stallion in his life. He had chivvied occasional inoffensive geldings without the will to resist, and he had lorded it over his mares.

Rory pawed the ground with heavy strokes, sending great clouds of dust streaming over his body. He changed his action, and the other forefoot raked billows above him. Bluff Downs pounded the earth, accepting the challenge.

Suddenly both horses stopped. For five seconds they stood, eyes reddened and flashing, lips snarling, and grinning teeth bared.

Bluff Downs lowered his head and sniffed the

ground. He snorted in great gusts which raised twin spirals of dust to his ears. He wheeled and spun, and lashed in anger at the spurts his breath had raised.

Rory pecked at a twig lying on the ground. He took it between his lips and nibbled it with his teeth. He played with it before tossing it aside; then he pawed the dust again.

Bluff Downs advanced to meet his challenger. With high-held head, arched neck and sweeping tail, with stertorous snorts and heaving flanks, with ears pricked and muscles drawn, mincingly and daintily he went to battle. He knew—he must have known—death rode in the air and destruction hovered above his shoulders.

As eagerly, if not so daintily, Rory advanced. He may not have had a creed handed him by long lineage. He was only a horse, a stallion with all the instinct and desires of his kind. That instinct was to take what he sought; if need be, to fight to the death.

They came together, slowly, watchfully, alert and poised. Each horse had his neck arched and his head bowed until his nostrils were almost touching his own chest. Their ears overlapped as they brought their nostrils together.

Bluff Downs swung away with a jerk and reared. Rory stood still. Bluff Downs dropped to the earth again. There was an etiquette of battle. The preliminaries must be complete before war commenced. Bluff Downs touched nostrils with Rory again, each flank heaving to the deep-drawn breaths.

Then deep and hoarse and hateful Rory yelled, his great voice smothering the shriller neigh of the smaller stallion. On the instant, while their breaths and voices were mingling, both horses reared. The preliminaries were complete. The battle had begun.

As they reared each horse pawed blindly, their forelegs interlocking in the effort, and each, snake-like, warded off; the striking teeth were parried, hot breaths mingling and hoarse screams sounding together.

They dropped to the ground, spun on front legs, and with lightning swiftness lashed with grass-skimming kicks.

They wheeled again and charged. The impact brought Rory up abruptly and sent Bluff Downs reeling. Rory shook in his stride—nothing more—and like a stabbing flame followed his staggering opponent. Bluff Downs dived under that charge, and his teeth sank in Rory's foreleg. He bunched himself, his muscles creaking, and desperately he strove to lift and throw.

The other horse was too heavy, too massive and too strong. He merely swung his head, and with a tearing chop ripped the chestnut from shoulder to chest. A great gash showed, a stream of red pulsed and flowed to the ground.

Rory rushed again. But the smaller horse was too quick. His charge was complete before Rory had well commenced. He swung in like a dazzling streak. His teeth chopped together on Rory's ribs. He jerked back, torn flesh and writhing sinews trailing from his teeth. In the same action he spun and lashed with his hind heels, thunderbolts which took the big fellow fairly under the belly.

Bluff Downs reared again, struck and held with his teeth. He took Rory along the crest and worried as a dog shakes a rat.

The mares watched. Perhaps they knew they were the prize.

Bluff Downs broke free. Like the snap of a flicking whip he darted in, raking Rory's ribs with his tearing fangs. As his teeth clicked together he spun and lashed with his hind hooves. He drove with all the venom, hate, implacable desire to kill, and all the weight and strength he had!

The bigger horse merely quivered, steadied himself and came at the charge again. Bluff Downs screamed, ranged up beside his foe, pounding hard and pounding often.

Rory was unused to this style of fighting. His confidence was shaken slightly, his temper frayed. He went berserk and roared in his fury. He forced the smaller horse back, leaning over him and pressing him down with his weight.

Bluff Downs faltered as a pebble turned under his hoof. He tripped, stumbled, with a wriggling action sought to break clear.

Rory swooped. His teeth closed on the chestnut's wither. He tore through skin, through flesh; his teeth found bone! He lifted Bluff Downs from the ground, shook him, swung him.

Rory's teeth closed on the piece he had taken. He shook again, and with a snap Bluff Downs dropped, a full mouth-size piece clean taken from his pouring wither. Before he had touched the ground, Rory wheeled and sent both heels ripping under his belly.

In a crumpled heap Bluff Downs fell to the ground. He gasped for breath, struggled convulsively. Over his heart, where the last kick had landed, one jagged bit of a broken rib stood out clear of his body. Under the torn skin and pulped flesh two other rib-ends stuck upright, and from a puncture where the broken points entered the chest slow blood was flowing.

Rory turned to the mares. He called, walked towards them, whinnying his love message to them. He extended his nostrils to touch those of the mare Sarah, who came to him.

Bluff Downs staggered to his feet. His tail hung listlessly, dragging between his hocks. His loins were arched. His breath came in gulps. Slowly the blood dripped from him, and he moved stiffly, unevenly and uncertainly, when he walked.

Sarah squealed again, and Bluff Downs lifted his low-hung head. Rory yelled once more, and Sarah's soft squeal, which preceded complete surrender, sounded to the stricken horse.

Bluff Downs charged! In a whirlwind of passion he came to the attack. He reared, and in his madness the greater strength of the other horse wilted before him. He screamed, striking, tearing and stabbing. He fastened his teeth in Rory's wither. He shook and worried, and the other horse stood firm as a rock. Bluff Downs reared again. He smashed with his fore hooves. He dropped to the ground as Rory reared and his teeth closed on the big fellow's foreleg.

Rory squealed in fear. He lunged across to catch that elusive wraith and Bluff Downs slipped under the attack and reared again. He gripped Rory's wither, slightly behind the apex, and the big horse cringed as those stabbing teeth sank in. He wriggled to get away, swinging his hindquarters.

As he swung a smashing hoof struck fairly on his loin-coupling. Something cracked, broke. Rory dropped helpless to the earth, his hindquarters trailing behind him, and with a jar Bluff Downs's hooves came to the ground as the horse sank beneath him.

Rory attempted to rise, his front legs stuck in front of him, his hindquarters flaccid and limp. Screaming his hate, Bluff Downs charged again. He battered the horse to the ground, pounded him, ripping with his teeth and smashing with his hooves. Rory struggled, wilted, sank to the ground and lay supine.

Bluff Downs turned to his brood. He was sick, sore, stricken to death, and perhaps he knew it. Also he knew, and this was his creed: He must assert his breeding. He owned that mob. He had to assert that ownership. He moved about them. He held his head high, extended his nostrils to Cascade.

Even as he caressed the mare there came a sharp tightening in his chest. He fought for his breath. He reared, struggling against that suffocation. As the blood gushed to his throat he fell at her feet.

For a few seconds he struggled, heaving in great strains for small gasps of air. Then, with a final convulsion, he lay still.

Chapter 6

A FLOOD OF COMMISERATION FLOWED IN ON KILGOUR when the death of Bluff Downs became known. Trouble did not stop at that. Cascade blundered through a fence one night and was killed. Kilgour brought Amathea in and turned her loose in the big horse paddock at the homestead.

Evans sent immediately and removed his two mares Linen Duster and Sethia, and Red Dick got gloriously drunk. Between drinks, interspersed with hiccups and profanity, he vowed he would not pay for the repairs to the fence. He cursed the whole thing as a dirty capitalistic trick to keep the worker down.

Fatter Singh wasted three days looking for his strayed bull camel. Then, with the fatalism of his class, he took the remainder of his team and his shoddy wares elsewhere. He would get the bull some other time. There was plenty of camel feed on Meetucka. Why worry?

"There's a bit of a silver lining behind the cloud," Kilgour assured himself with a show of optimism. "There's worse things can happen a station than to get a change of stallions."

By letter he learned what Head Office thought on the matter.

We note with regret that Bluff Downs has been killed in a fight with another stallion. We recognize, of course, that this was an accident which could not be foreseen or prevented, and we do not in any way attribute any blame to you. At the present time, unfortunately, it is not suitable to us to send another stallion to replace Bluff Downs, even though we recognize that the horse numbers must be kept up to the requisite standard for the efficient working of the property. Mr. Peter Outhwaite informs us that he has a colt on Meetucka, by Bluff Downs from Susette, who should now be about two years old, fit to work lightly with a limited number of good mares. We recommend that you utilize this colt for a few years. He, as you know, is magnificently bred. He should suit the purpose. As you have no Bluff Downs mares yet fit to go to the stud for breeding purposes, there is no danger of inbreeding. Tooley Street, which, as you know, is the name Mr. Outhwaite has given his colt, could run with the mares which constituted Bluff Downs's stud.

Under the formal signature of the company there was a pencil-scribbled P.S. in Peter Outhwaite's handwriting:

Hard luck, George. It must have been a gorgeous fight and the little fellow died game. I wish I could have seen it. Give

Tooley a square go. I know you'd sooner have another horse of different breeding. I'll try and get you one as soon as possible. But, man, times are tight. Now Bluff Downs is dead I'll arrange to get Susette and her colt here as soon as possible. My respectful salaams to Mrs. Kilgour, and kiss yourself good-night for me.—P.O.

"That's that!" Kilgour muttered. "And, that being that, it is that!"

"The idea's right enough in theory," he continued. Really, it's good. I suppose one strain won't do too much harm; but I wouldn't like to run on with it. Locally-bred stallions in a district that has distinct seasons, a regular rainfall, frost during the winter, and a few other things, is right in moderation. Locally-bred stallions in the dry west, where the heat saps vitality, and the seasons ain't regular, is courting disaster. Apart from that, I'm doubtful about this joker. His breeding's right; his make and shape's right; every external part of him fills the bill. But, I don't know. His ma and his pa didn't mesh, for one thing. We'll see."

Tooley Street was brought up from the bullock paddock and put with the mares in Mingeri. He behaved like an adolescent schoolboy suddenly transplanted into a Mothers' Union meeting. He was shy; he was diffident; he attempted to hide his shyness and fear under an assumed air of bluster. He raked up the dust and squealed. He wheeled about him and lashed at the dust he had raised.

When a wise old mare, mother of many, came near him with her ears lopped, he dropped his masculine pose: he forgot to pretend he was the lord of the mob, and sidled away from the punishment which that old mare would mete out to him. Instead of demanding what he considered were his rights—as his sire did—he humbly besought favours. He was weak, and the brood fell to pieces under that slack reign. They roamed about the paddock in twos and threes, only coming near the colt when it suited their purpose.

"He's only a boy yet," Kilgour commented. "If he takes after his dad he'll spring them old ladies to attention."

Kilgour had Amathea brought in from the spell paddock and put among the workers. She was nervous in that strange, grown company. Odd tufts of hair were lifted from her quarters, an occasional mark of raking teeth along her ribs proved that the others were putting her in her place and making her thoroughly at home. She was run up to the yards every morning, pairing with old Roan, the biggest and sleepiest draughthorse on the place, standing head-and-tail with him while they switched flies from each other's faces.

Kilgour commenced to handle her, taking that on himself as a labour of love.

Amathea started when his hand was placed on her neck. But there was a comforting feeling about that firm stroking, a soothing sound about the low rumble of words which came to her. The sweat sprang from her, she twitched her ears nervously; but she was not really afraid. She had to submit—there was no getting away from it—and, being gifted with a modicum of ordinary horse sense, she submitted.

After half an hour's handling, when the filly had grown accustomed to all sorts of liberties being taken with her, a halter was slipped over her head. She fought against that in futile protest, but half-heartedly.

Then the gate at the end of the crush was opened and she bounded out. But even as she thought she was free her head and neck were jerked round, and the man on the end of the halter rope forced her to face him. That new experience of being captive and yet free took some time to reach her understanding. She fought it—strenuously and wholeheartedly—without avail.

"Steady, the little mare!" The rumbling voice continued, carrying with it a note of assurance and comfort. "Steady, th' filly."

The man stood close, rubbing his body against hers. He fondled and caressed her with his hands. He walked about her, never taking his hands off her when near her. He let her go, advanced to her again. She tried to escape, but the trailing rope which the man carried always brought her to him again. The lesson was repeated and repeated, until finally she stood to be caught, did not flinch at his advance, even reciprocated some of the friendship offered her. She rubbed her head against the man's body.

"That'll do you for to-day, old girl."

Next day he taught her to lead. With a length of light rope looped over her loins and dangling about her hocks, he stood in front of her, holding both that line and the halter shank. "T'ck!" he clicked, pulling on the shank and jerking the hock line at the same time. The filly leant to the pull of the shank, and when the snap twanged against her hocks she bounded forward.

"Steady, the little mare!" the man crooned to her. "That's the good little mare! That's the way to do it, old girl! Come on, Amie, we'll do it again. You'll learn to lead in no time with this."

Half a dozen jerks of the line made her spring forward each time, to be met with exaggerated praise and soothing patting. She learned to associate the pull of the shank with the snap of the line. She anticipated the snap by going to the pull. In half an hour she was leading freely wherever the man took her, and the loop on her loins was lying slack, merely as an emergency.

Then Kilgour picked up her feet. Standing beside her shoulder he rubbed his leg against her near foreleg. When she was used to that he cleverly hooked the toe of his boot under her fetlock. He lifted. The first few attempts were failures. The mare plunged away. But she grew accustomed to it. Then the man leant down and picked up her hoof with his hand. She fought against that. Rather, she tried to fight. The man cunningly held only the toe of her hoof in his finger and thumb. Try as she would, she could not put any weight into her struggles. That double-bent joint numbed her muscles. She could only swing her leg blindly, aimlessly and without effect. She recognized the futility of that. She ceased to struggle.

He did the other foreleg, then handled her hindquarters, running his hand down her hocks. If Amathea asked herself a question, it assuredly was: Why struggle against kindness, and why combat friendship? She did neither.

Kilgour invited his wife to the yards to have a look at the filly. Mrs. Kilgour was plump, matronly, and to a certain extent easy-going.

"Amathea, is it, George?" she asked. "Well, if you'll promise to stop singing her praises to me, I'll go with you."

They walked to the yards. Kilgour ran the filly out by herself.

"What do you think of that?" he asked, placing his hand on Amathea's neck and fondling her.

"Is that Amathea?" Mrs. Kilgour asked. "I thought you said she was a beautiful filly!"

"Ain't she?"

"But she's too ragged, George," his wife complained. "She's too long and lean. I don't like her face, either. It's too long. I suppose she's right enough in her way; but I wouldn't call her pretty. She's not nearly round enough to be pretty."

"Well, I'll be frizzled!" ejaculated Kilgour. "This ain't a rocking-horse or a circus pony, Nell. This is the makings of a working stock-horse. This is the sort of thing that don't get out in the limelight, that don't hear the cheering and applause, and that props up the Empire from behind, as it were. Why, if the poet laureate was a horseman, he'd sit down here and now and compose an Iliad about this thing. I can nearly write poetry about her myself."

Chapter 7

AMATHEA WAS TURNED OUT IN GUMBOIL PADDOCK with all the other weaners of the year. In addition, Gumboil was used as a spell paddock for the station's workers; the growers and unbroken stuff ran there, and it was the general horse paddock for all but a few special classes. Parrot Creek ran along the frontage, with holes lasting up to four months after the rains. At the back was the Gumboil Bore—a sub-artesian, equipped with a windmill, tank and troughs.

The thirty-odd thousand acres of Gumboil Paddock constituted ideal horse-growing country. Rich in Mitchell and Flinders grasses and well sprinkled with saltbush, those pebbly downs kept the horses' feet trimmed, chipping off pieces, giving them a hardness of flint.

The water from the bore, though with a certain

brackishness which made it unpalatable to men, was
appreciated by the horses. It was good stock water. The
variety of feed gave them endless picking and the
change which their systems desired. The scope of those
limitless acres gave them room to expand—to race and
play, to grow and develop.

The rains came. The flies and other pests of the air
herded the horses together in one mob; it was torture
for an animal to go away by itself. The youngsters
learned the benefit of the fly-ring. They understood
the meaning of an older horse lopping its ears and
rolling the whites of its eyes. The yearlings had all
the bumptious cocksureness which is the privilege of
growing stock of any class of animal—from mankind
down. But they also assimilated a little wisdom with it.

Trouble came to some of the older horses—those
whose skins were tender, and who had not the vitality
of youth to combat the attacks of diseases and wounds.
During the height of the fly season they developed
great sores on their hips. The mob was mustered to the
yard, the injured ones taken out and dressed with a
mixture of Stockholm tar and flour and the lot were
returned to Gumboil. They were seen at least once a
fortnight.

But the flies did not last for ever. With the richness of the feed following the rains, and the variety
of it, even they could not prevent the horses from putting on condition and getting foolishly fat. They could
not stop the young stock growing. When the flies eased
sufficiently to allow the mob to split and mate according to its individual and collective desires the animals

spread in twos, threes, a half-dozen or more—batches all over the paddock.

Amathea became mates with half a dozen youngsters, of both sexes, of about her own age. They had nothing to do but preserve their health and grow.

They played. They evolved all sorts of new games. They found, by standing on the ridge just below Corkscrew Bend, they could see a long line of the road running from Iladda to the head station. They used to spend hours watching that road. Suddenly, away in the distance, a ribbon of dust would be seen rising. That would be a car or some other vehicle on the road. Immediately, and with no audible warning being given, they would gather on top of the ridge, watch the rising ribbon of dust drawing nearer. Their eyes would be glistening, they would quiver with nervous anticipation and shiver with the delight of dread. Then, when the suspense began to irritate them, they would slyly nip one another, kick lightly and skirmish a little.

The car, the buggy, the wagon, the horseman, or whatever it might be, would come into sight and draw abreast. One or two would break in pretended fear, scampering away nervously, only to wheel back and rejoin the others. Suddenly the whole lot would wheel, race, twist and dodge, bucking and bounding, each going its separate way. They would pivot on their hindlegs, wheel and snort wildly in pretended challenge. Then they would come together again and look for more horrors to burst on them.

There was another game at the waterholes in the creek when there was water in those holes. The main feature of that game was to make the water as muddy as possible, to paw and stir it to a floating soup, before lying and rolling in it. That was a great old game if the water was low and others were just coming in for a clean drink.

There were a thousand games, each of them good, but none to equal that mad race in the early morning when the air was sharp and crisp, when any position served as a starting-place and any old where was the winning-post.

The youngsters were yarded periodically when spelling horses were wanted for working purposes. They knew what it was to race to the yard, prop, rear and squeal at the entrance gates, and then take position inside and doze placidly. Occasionally a couple of three-year-olds would be drafted out and kept to be broken.

Every time they came to the yard, after he had looked over the other horses, Kilgour would run Amathea out and catch her. If he had the time to spare he would lead her around a little and pick up her feet. But he always caught her, even if it was only to pat her roughly, mumble a few words of endearment, and, in the language of the stockyards, tell her a tale.

Down in Mingeri Tooley Street was growing to maturity. His first batch of foals from the old mares he had in Bullock Paddock were admired. The first foals of any new horse, when they are young, and if the sire himself has any quality at all, are always admired.

The horse and his batch of mares were to be mustered for the foals to be branded and weaned, according to their ages. Kilgour went with Harry and a couple of other men to bring the stallion to the yards at the head station. There were thirty mares. Tooley Street kept twenty of them with him. The other ten were scattered about the paddock in several lots. Those outsiders showed scars along their ribs and torn ribbons of hair from off their rumps.

"He's got his likes and his dislikes," Kilgour observed. "A young fellow like him shouldn't be vicious like that. Susette was a sweet-tempered thing. His sire had a temper, but he wasn't mean."

When the outsiders were run to the mob Tooley Street came out to meet them. He was a magnificent specimen of his breed, though he lacked the finish which only maturity would give. He stood about fifteen one, long, low, well coupled and superbly sprung, in spite of his youth. His chestnut coat glittered like the flames of a fire. He was every inch a stallion as he posed in front of the approaching mares.

Tooley Street tired of posing before his brood. He turned to the mounted men who were watching him. Some evil thought filtered through his mind, and suddenly his eyes reddened and his ears lopped. He swung towards Harry Peelben, head lowered to near ground level, the whites of his eyes showing, his ears laid back along his neck, and his lips curled. He slid over the ground with an action that was snake-like, and he swung his head in the manner of a snake about to strike.

"This is the first test," Kilgour thought. "And he couldn't have picked a better man to try it against!

Now we'll see whether this fellow's a real horse, or whether he's an imitation of nothing done up in hide."

As the horse swung towards him Harry loosed his whip. It was not the twenty-foot thong beloved of fiction writers. It was not even capable of "delivering a death-blow." It was only an eight-foot thing, thirty-inch fall and twenty-inch handle. That, roughly, gave the man a radius of about eleven feet. It gave him a whip which was fast and, provided the man could use it, one which would do all that any whip could do. Harry could use a whip!

Like a lick of lightning the stallion struck towards the man. He was puzzled, and perhaps slightly cowed, by the fact that the man ignored the attack. When a mere eight feet separated them, he swung aside and swept past. He squealed his anger, shuffled his hindquarters and lashed.

Squeal was cut short and kick never delivered. Searing lightning bit his rump and thunder cracked above him. At the actual moment of impact the man drew the lash slightly, rasping the fall on the skin of the horse. A red weal sprang and slow dribbles of blood formed.

The stallion bounded in the air. While he was off the ground fire took him under the flank and across the bare skin of his belly, and the snapping report of a gun burst beneath him!

Harry coiled his whip. Tooley Street charged among his mares. He took Sarah by the nape of the neck between his teeth and tossed her to one side. He chopped Vashtai, and a wound opened on her hip. He lashed Clementine, and he kicked blindly. He surged through them, brushing them aside and chopping. He reared and smashed a foal to the ground, leaving the small body twitching. He raced to the lead and blocked the mob. He cut out Sheba and chased her round one wing, keeping her out when she tried to race back, and he lifted a flap of skin from Una's ribs as he passed.

"Hey!" a voice roared, accompanied by the report of a whip.

Tooley Street stopped in his tracks. Almost he cowered; then he slunk among the mares and hid himself in the midst of them.

"P'sst!" Kilgour spat his disgust. "You've given me a rotten taste in the mouth."

He rode over to a tree, broke a bit of a stick about three feet in length and idly trimmed it with his knife as he rode across to Harry.

"Good work," he said briefly, without emotion.

Chapter 8

EARLY IN MARCH, WHILE THE WET SEASON WAS STILL in progress, Amathea was taken to the head station to be broken. She was just three years old. But for the development which maturity would bring, she was full grown. She was a truly glorious mare, and Kilgour, as he walked about her, voiced his comments.

"You're Stockwell right through, old girl. At least, you're what we're led to believe is the Stockwell touch. So you should be! You've got more of his blood than anything else."

Harry broke the mare. That was comparatively easy; she had been so well handled. But she showed spirit that pleased Kilgour when Harry slipped her tail through the loop of the crupper. That was a new sensation for her. She kicked in vigorous protest, and when she kicked and stretched herself the girth pinched her. She snapped her head down between her knees, humped her back until the crupper strap stood taut as a fiddle string, jammed her tail between her legs, swelled her muscles until overlying flesh hid the girths, and in the flash of a second she leapt in the air. She landed stiff-legged with a jarring thud, sprang again, turned on her side in the air—known as "floating"—and, after a repetition in reverse, she landed with the near shoulder tucked under. She did not spring from there; she just bounced, and with a cat-like wriggle and squirm landed with her off-shoulder grazing the ground. She plunged round the yard in high leaps and, her fighting spirit roused, roared her anger.

Kilgour's thoughts were too jumbled to express. They amounted to something like: "Oh, you gem! You ain't any flaccid nothing that submits to everything. Look at the way she picks herself up when she rises! Look at the neat way she lands! A horse that bucks must have strength and muscular development. It must have balance. It must be able to stand on its feet. If it's got breeding as well there's no telling what that horse mightn't do. But it must be clean bucking—whips of devil and devoid of vice. This thing's got the lot. You little beauty!"

To Harry, he merely remarked casually, "She handles herself well, Harry."

"Um-m-m," Harry grunted in affirmation. "I like to see 'em show what's in 'em. This is goin' to be a good mare, Mr. Kilgour."

Kilgour's Mare

Harry soothed her, adjusted the bearing reins. There was nothing more to be done for a couple of hours. She had to break herself in some respects. Harry left the yards to attend to other work.

Later, Harry drove her in reins, messed about her and indulged to the full his fancies of what constituted perfect breaking—and every worthwhile horseman is full to the brim with fancies of that sort. He led her on horseback, then put his saddle and gear on her for the first riding. He mounted her in the big yard.

The filly flinched, swayed to balance the unaccustomed weight, and stood still. The man hit her down the ribs with a short length of rubber hosing. That made a resounding smack, hurt not at all, lifted no hair and caused no bruises. But its unexpectedness caused the mare to bound forward. She hit the ground stiff-legged to commence the bucking which would dislodge the weight on her back. But she swayed when she landed. Instead of springing in the air she had to balance herself. She gave a half-hearted bound and plodded stolidly forward every time she was urged.

"Are you right, Harry?" Kilgour called, opening the gate.

"Right."

Kilgour mounted his old horse, swung it into the yard and ranged up beside the filly. He rode across to the open gate, partly coaxing and partly forcing the novice towards it. They went out in the open. Amathea felt confidence in having a horse beside her, and went more freely. They did figures of eight about the flat. She was coaxed into a trot. When she stretched to the canter the girths pinched her again. She snapped herself together in a tight ball and tried to buck. But she could not balance the weight on top of her.

In less than half an hour she seemed to be stretching to her work with confidence, apparently enjoying it, beginning to recognize and respond to the directions from the reins and the swing of the thighs.

Amathea went out in the camp when the season broke and learnt to do the light work which is handed young things. She learnt quickly that it was futile to plunge against the restraint the hobbles imposed; she learnt to shuffle along in the short-stepped gait forced by them; and she recognized that when a man approached her, bent double and with his hand extended, it was wise to stand—that the man was about to release her from the shackles of the hobbles.

Particularly she learnt the value of smoke. When the first tinge of dawn came, and sandflies woke to their work, then a wisp of smoke rising in the distance was a haven of refuge. The horses would stand in that, the thicker and more stifling the better. She learnt to balance her rider subconsciously. She learnt to watch the cattle she was working. Almost, it seemed, she took a delight in the work.

Towards the end of April she was turned out for her first spell. She ignored her old and unbroken mates in Gumboil. Rather, on a new standing and a higher social level, she preferred to mix with the workers from the camp which had also been turned out to spell. The view of the road from Corkscrew Bend now held no allurements for her. With Breakspear, Maureen, Dandy and Sassafras she fed on the flat out from Duck Hole.

The Iladda Picnic Club held its annual meeting on 24 May. The club had grown. It was influential. The best elements of the district controlled it. It had a waiting list.

As the annual meeting was dated to fit in after the first general musters of the year, and before the bullock musters started, all stations attended in force. Evans was there, in his string two Bluff Downs youngsters—those from Sethia and Linen Duster.

"But they're only babies, Evans," Kilgour complained. "Why, they're only three!"

"Every horse that wins a Derby is only three," Evans retorted. "Many of them win Melbourne Cups at that age, too."

Kilgour agreed. It was hardly worth while pointing out that a Derby winner at three was forced, grown and matured to equal a bush horse of five.

"I had this colt of Sethia's, Set Down, broken in as a two-year-old. He is set," Evans continued. "Dust Down, the filly from Linen Duster, was broken in even earlier. In fact, I can't say exactly when she was broken. I took no chances with her. She was too good to take chances with. You might say she's been broken in from the time she was weaned."

"You might be right," Kilgour said agreeably. "Still, I prefer to let 'em develop under natural conditions."

Set Down started in the Breeders' Plate. He galloped like a half-grown pup. His legs seemed to tangle themselves, and he sprawled all over the course.

"He hasn't got the strength and muscular development to hold himself together," was Kilgour's verdict.

Dust Down started in the big race of the first day, The Bachelor's Bag. She bounded out at flagfall and sped ahead of the field like a startled rabbit. Literally, she was bolting, and it was only the horror of those thundering hooves behind her which kept her going.

One horse caught and passed her. Dust Down swerved and flinched. The rest of the field swung on her, engulfed her. She came out of the tail end of them wallowing in her stride and struggling hopelessly in pursuit.

"That thing has pace," Evans exclaimed at Kilgour's side. "She gets it from her mother. If she only had her mother's stamina she'd be a champion. I think she's short of a gallop. Did you see the way she shut up?"

"If she was mine, and Set Down was mine," Kilgour said tartly, "I'd take 'em straight home and turn 'em out in the biggest paddock I had. I wouldn't let any one look at 'em, let alone touch 'em, until the end of next March. That's what I'd do with 'em."

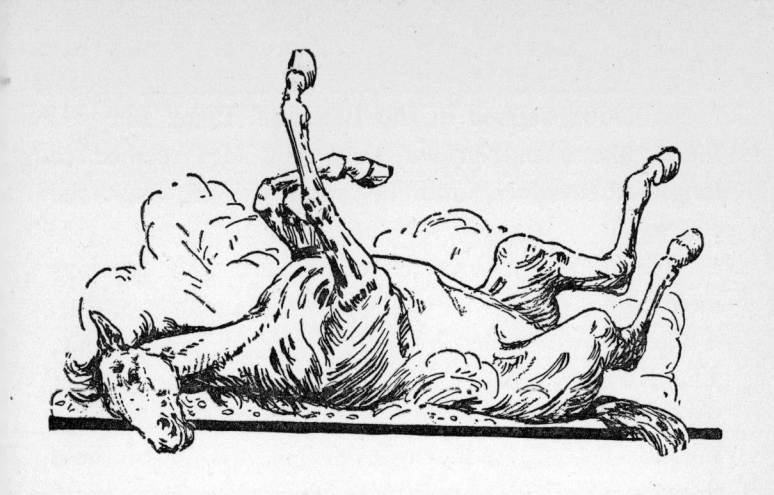

Chapter 9

AFTER AMATHEA HAD BEEN IN THE CAMP A MONTH Harry decided to take her to the head station. He reached the homestead late in the afternoon, when the westering sun threw grotesque and mile-long shadows, and white ribbons of birds in flight streamed through the air and converged on central points as the corellas flew to their communal camp. The wind blew endlessly from the south-east, a clean wind, dry, brittle and sparkling with life.

Harry's mount, Membrane, swung along confidently towards the yards, picking her feet up cleanly and moving smartly with the action which all horses show when going to a well-known spot. Amathea, with only a halter on her, and with the shank lightly held, ran beside the ridden mare, head high.

As Harry reached the yards, and just as he was

about to dismount, Kilgour rode in. He had been out round the Knob, through Balana Plains, and over by the Sprinkler Bore, having a look at the country, viewing the state of the stock—and enjoying the whole process.

"G'day, Harry," he said, dismounting beside his head stockman. "What's up?"

"Nothin'," Harry replied. "I'm camped at th' Weaner Yards. We'll be shiftin' down Pituri in th' mornin'. Before I went down th' bottom end I thought I'd bring this filly in. You want her, don't you?"

"What's wrong with her, Harry?"

"Nothin'. I only thought you wanted her."

"I thought you'd keep her longer," Kilgour replied, standing beside Amathea and commencing the game with her which all young horses love to play endlessly. He put the flat of the palm of his hand across her lips, muzzling her, and tickled the side of her mouth with his middle finger. Immediately the mare reached forward, palpitating her lips, trying to take the flat hand in her teeth.

"She's quiet now," Harry replied evenly.

"What's wrong with her?" Kilgour repeated, letting the mare's teeth push his hand away and then muzzling her again.

"Nothin's wrong with her."

"Then why'd you bring her in?"

"Because, Mr. Kilgour, this is th' daddy of all mares! You never seen a thing come quicker to its work. She likes it. A man don't have to ride her—she carries him along."

"Buck at all, Harry?"

"Never humped her back. But by th' feel of th' strength an' balance of her, if she does buck she'll buck bad."

"And you expect an old cove like me to ride a raw filly!" Kilgour said in mock surprise. "Here it is, the middle of winter, when all youngsters are a bit tight when they're saddled, and you spring a soothing tale of a rare buckjumper on me and tell me there's no need to worry. If she slings me I'll have to send her back to you again. Then it's going to take you twelve months to reform her. By that time you'll be fond of her. If I want her there's going to be a row—in fact, I'll either have to do without my mare or get a new head stockman. Ain't that the way it goes?"

"Oh, no," Harry grinned, knowing the boss had touched the fact of it. "This mare won't sling you."

"I'll see she don't!" Kilgour said with emphasis. "Are you staying here to-night? How about giving her a ride for me in the morning, when it's raw and cold?"

"I got cattle in hand at th' yards," said Harry, showing without the necessity of further words that he had to return to the camp. "I'll come up in th' mornin' an' rough her for you if you like."

"It's all right," Kilgour laughed. "Don't you worry about me. I'm old enough to look after myself." He changed the subject. "Old Wally Budd'll be here about Wednesday week—you know, the buyer for the Domestic and Meat Export Company. You'll have all the bullocks and fat cows in hand, will you? I'll bring him down to the camp. You'll be ready, eh? Good egg! Well, I suppose you'll be having a feed before you go back to the camp, Harry."

Next day Kilgour walked to the yards. Woppida was there. The boss's boy, he devoted his days to showing a spurious eagerness for work between the hours of just after breakfast and the morning smoko. For the rest of the day his sole ambition was to keep out of sight, dodge the boss, and evade work. Considering the fact that he was only an untutored aborigine, he was wonderfully successful.

"Hey, Woppida," Kilgour hailed him. "Come here. You've got to act as my wet nurse. Does that weigh on you?"

"Huh-ha," Woppida agreed, and grinned.

He saw his boss was in a good humour. The best reply was a laugh. Woppida laughed.

"Every time mine catch-it that one chestnut mare, that one Amathea, you been get-em 'nother horse an' come belong-it me," Kilgour directed him. "Every time, now. Suppose-em you don't, s'elp me goodness, I'll skin you alive!"

Woppida caught enough of the drift of the order to be impressed.

Kilgour drafted four horses, including Amathea, into the round yard. He separated her, letting the others run out of the open gate. They slipped through and stood in the pound yard adjoining and Kilgour stood in the open gateway.

Amathea was restless. She objected to being in the yard alone. Her mates were in the next yard and the gate between them was open. She was inclined to go

to them. But the man stood in that gateway! She
swung around the yard a couple of times restlessly,
edging towards the open gate and her mates, and
sheering off when she came near the man.

A couple of times Kilgour walked to the mare,
petted her, coaxed her and soothed her. Each time, as
soon as he turned to go back to the open gate she was
inclined to go towards it. But she would not come to
him, coax her as he might.

He got a handful of small pebbles. When the mare
turned from him, and when she showed no desire to
work towards the gate, he flicked a small pebble at her
and stirred her into uneasiness. Each time she turned
to him again, and every time she advanced half a step
towards him, the man went to her and recommenced
his petting and exaggerated coaxings.

At last she came straight up to him. She did not
come because she wanted to come. She came because
she was irritated by pebbles if she stood in the far side
of the yard; also because her inclinations led her to
go to her mates, which were beyond the man and
through the open gate in which he stood.

"Well done, little mare!" Kilgour petted her effusively.

Of course he could have done the same thing with
a whip. He held that a whip's a damnable thing to use
on a young, or an old, horse; that it brings the vice
to the surface, frightens them.

He played with the mare till lunch-time.

He had no doubt about what Mrs. Kilgour's attitude would be towards his riding that young green mare. He kept the news till next morning. "Kiss me good-bye, Nell," he said then. "I'm riding Amathea to-day. I'm going round by Gumboil Bore and across to Tooringa. I don't know which way I'll go from there. But I'll be right; the guardian angel, Woppida, will be on the job."

"I wish you wouldn't joke of such things," Mrs. Kilgour said. "You'll take care of yourself, won't you?"

"Who—me? Let me tell you, Nell, when old George Kilgour's in danger I watch him closer than a brother. I've saved that old fool's life no end of times."

Whistling, but with an odd little quiver inside him which he would not like to try to explain, Kilgour went to the yards. He caught Amathea and saddled her.

"Steady, old girl," he murmured to her.

He thought: "I'm fifty. I'm not a has-been, but I ain't as good a man as I used to be. I'm not frightened, even if my nerves ain't as good as they were."

Amathea was a little agitated. It was a cold morning; she held herself stiffly; her muscles were drawn and tensed, and she moved in a proppy fashion— "tight," in the language of the stockyards.

He completed the saddling, slung the reins over the knee-pads, and let her go in the yard while he walked across and pretended to find fault with the way Woppida had saddled old Belsize. Amathea flinched from the girth, tightened herself for a second, then walked casually and freely about the yard, shaking her head in the automatic fashion in which western horses learn to ward off the flies.

Kilgour caught her and mounted. He thought: "I'm not frightened. It's just old nerves."

Amathea moved away freely, and with Woppida riding behind they passed the house. Kilgour would have given a pound to take his hat off and wave it. Instead, he rode past—interested in something over to the left.

They rode out through Gumboil. As they left the miles behind them the man and the mare seemed to breed a confidence between them. Amathea was swinging along, her tail swaying from side to side as she walked, her strides long and springy, and when she put her hind-foot down it was six inches ahead of the track left by the fore hoof on the same side.

Kilgour had dissolved and swallowed the distressing lump in his throat. He gloried in the action of the mare under him and the fact that he, old George Kilgour, was riding a young un that he had bred himself.

He thought: "I'm not in any hurry, but I've been fair dying to try this mare's canter for the past five miles, only I ain't been game to test it. It's got to come some time. Why not now?"

He gathered the reins together and leant forward slightly.

Amathea knew the meaning of that signal. She reached out in a canter. Her rider swayed to her action as she swept along. She stretched freely with her front legs and gathered her hind-legs under her, gripping the earth powerfully and springing forward. It was an effortless action. She seemed to draw distance to her, churn it into miles beneath her, and lay streams of them behind her. Further, and better, she was under perfect control and balance. She pricked her ears and looked about her. She took an interest and an apparent pleasure in what she was doing.

Suddenly she put her near fore hoof on a bit of rotten ground which crumbled under her. She tripped, quivered slightly and recovered, all in one action. But that sudden heave and strenuous effort jerked her rider slightly; the girths slipped and pinched. Amathea snapped at the bit, whipped her head down and gave four flying bucks straight ahead. That eased things for her and made everything comfortable again. She stretched once more to her flowing canter.

Kilgour thought that if he'd known it was coming he'd have fallen off with fright. As it was he had given a life-like imitation of a horseman.

After dinner at Tooringa they rode round the back of Mingeri and turned for home.

As he rode along Kilgour was thinking: "It's about forty miles. Fellows talk about riding a colt forty miles the day it's broken. That's a picture-book tale. If a colt was ridden that far the day he was broken, that would be the only day he'd ever do it—he'd be a useless frame from that on and for ever. Forty miles is a good day. Any decent horse ought to do it without turning a hair. Plenty can't—more's the pity. Still, with you only a youngster and me riding nearly thirteen stone all told, it's a good day for you. You ain't going to be pampered, lady. You're going to do your work. If you're good, I'll know it. By the way you're shaping now you're going to be what Harry said you were: the daddy of the lot."

"Hulloa!" he said aloud. "What's wrong now?"

Amathea had stiffened, drawn herself together. Her sensitive nostrils had picked up a dread taint before the blunter feelings of the man had become conscious of anything unusual. She shortened her stride, lifted her head, pricked her ears and snorted.

Then, as they swung round a clump of gidgee, the thing was plain: a wandering bull camel stood out from the shade, and the wind brought a strong whiff of the brute.

Belsize was old, seasoned, used to anything, and too sluggish to care. He plodded along, barely deigning to lift an ear or raise an eyelid. Amathea was young, sensitive, and her one and only previous meeting with a camel had left a lasting impression. She snatched at the bit, turned and attempted to race away. But strong thighs swung her; firm hands held the reins, and the crooning rumble, which she knew and was beginning to understand, sounded:

"Steady, the little mare. Steady, there. You ain't frightened, old woman! That's the style. Stick to it, girl!"

As Amathea neared the camel she was flaccid with terror. Gradually, slowly, she gathered confidence from the man who rode her. That strength gained her a new courage she did not feel, his will asserted itself and overcame her fear. She responded to the soothing calm of the man, braved the danger and passed it.

At the yard, where the horses were let go, Kilgour rubbed the mare's ears, took her muzzle in the crook of his arm, laid his cheek on hers and crooned to her. Then he stepped back and watched her as she trotted over to the dust patch out from the saddle-room.

Amathea lowered her head and sniffed. She turned a couple of times, bent at the knees and hocks. When her breast was about a foot from the ground she flopped to the earth with a satisfied grunt, stretched her neck out flat on the ground, rubbed her head backwards and forwards. With a heave and a twist she rolled over on her back, her four legs wriggling in the air with ecstatic pleasure. She rolled back again. Then, with a greater heave, she balanced on her back again, wavered for a second, rolled right over and rubbed her head and neck on the ground on that side of her body. She gave a couple more half-hearted heaves which did not get her more than half over. Then she placed her forelegs stiffly before her, gathered her hind-legs under her. With a lift and a strain she stood on her four feet, braced her legs widely, shook herself vigorously and freed her coat of dust, dry sweat and dirt.

Kilgour, watching her as she whinnied to her mates and trotted towards the creek, shifted his hat to one side and scratched his grizzled head. Quietly he asked himself: "I wonder if it'd be considered a sacrilege if a man offered up a bit of a prayer for the welfare of a mere horse?"

Chapter 10

AMATHEA'S EDUCATION CONTINUED. DURING THE breaking process she had been taught to stand where her reins were tied to any post, stick or limb of a tree.

She now had a new lesson. This was to learn to stand wherever and whenever her rider dismounted and dropped the reins over her head to the ground.

Kilgour used a bridle with an extra long pair of reins. He rode the mare away from the yards, and when distant less than half a mile, while her mates were still within clear view, he dismounted and dropped the reins over her head to the ground, then turned and walked briskly away from her.

Amathea swung and started to trot towards her mates feeding in the horse-paddock. She took about six steps, the loop of the reins trailing on the ground, and then she put a hoof on them. Her action snagged the reins and snapped the bit in her mouth. She threw her head up, jerked and bounded. That released the rein from under her hoof and she was free. But every few strides the same thing happened again. Finally, the loop of the reins slipped over her hoof and locked itself under her fetlock joint.

Kilgour went to her, petted her effusively. So the lesson went on till Amathea knew, definitely, that the reins trailing on the gound were as sure a tie as any halter attached to any stout post.

Mustering cattle down Pituri, Kilgour mounted Amathea. He rode slowly from the men before they had saddled their horses. A hundred yards clear of them he dismounted, dropped the reins to the ground, left the mare standing and hurried back to his swag. He unrolled it hastily, rapidly searching for nothing, with one eye all the time on the mare standing out on the flat.

She never moved; even when the mounted men rode round her on their way out to the cattle she merely shuffled uneasily.

"Th' boss's showin' off." Harry grinned at the man beside him. "He's fair married to that mare. An' he's doin' pretty good work on her, too! He's goin' to be terrible pleased when I ask him to take a cut this afternoon."

Kilgour remounted and caught up with his head stockman.

"I thought I'd left that notebook at home," he explained.

"That mare stands good," said Harry.

"Don't she? Ain't she a gem, Harry! Really, that was only a bit of kidstakes about me rushing to the swag. I've been training this mare, Harry. I wanted to see if she'd stand. But a man would look a fool doing it without some reason, wouldn't he?"

"Um-m-m!" Harry agreed. "I made sure you'd forgotten somethin'. I thought you'd been bitten by a snake, you was so terrible busy."

Kilgour rode round the camp of cattle, pretending to look at them, wanting his head stockman to invite him to take his mare in and cut out some bullocks. That was the higher art. He wanted to test Amathea. He could hint that he would like to do it; he might insist that he should do it; but the observance of unwritten rules of etiquette helped to make work run smoothly. The head stockman was in charge of the camp. The manager could direct the camp as a whole; but to the head stockman was reserved the right of individual direction.

As Kilgour quickly noted, there were only from twenty to thirty bullocks in that mob to cut out and put with the fats. The men, used to working together, fell into place without any orders. Charlie and Joe rode round the tail to steady the back of the camp; Mick and Billy worked on the face of each wing; Terry took the middle of the face and Andy waited to hold the cut. Harry, riding Splinter, rode into the camp to commence cutting out. Kilgour hovered about, working round the cattle, and finally took station on the face.

Amathea was palpably excited. She may not have known the work, but in her breeding were many sires who were noted progenitors of stock-horses. Some instinct told her it was her work, the labour for which she had been bred, and the little taste of it she had been given before Harry had returned her to the head station had whetted her appetite for some more. She held her head high, her ears pricked. When her rider reined her to a standstill she pawed the earth in her impatience.

Harry commenced the cut. Splinter, wise old camp horse that he was, made play of those quiet-running bullocks. One, two, three, four, five, six came out. Kilgour counted them. Harry took out another four.

Kilgour, impatient to take a cut, flashed Amathea past Harry on the face, taking the cut from him and showing his easy mastery of the mare. He pulled her back on her haunches and wheeled her on a pin's head. He would have indignantly denied any charge that he was showing off.

Harry came out of the camp and rode across to his boss.

"They're runnin' pretty good, Mr. Kilgour," he said. "Ol' Splinter don't seem to be workin' too well. I think he's a bit lame. He might be wantin' a bit of a spell. That Amathea's pretty handy. Would you take them ten or a dozen what's left?"

"H'm-m-m," Kilgour assented. "I saw the old fellow wasn't doing too well. It's a shame to sour a good horse, Harry. I'll take that dozen or so out sooner than see a good horse cruelled."

Amathea stepped proudly among the cattle. Perhaps she was a shade nervous, a little frightened. But she went bravely, picking her way carefully, her ears pricked confidently. She gained confidence from the strong thighs which held her, from the firm hands which guided her. She walked through the cattle.

Kilgour spotted the bullock he wanted. He dropped his hands level with the pommel of the saddle, drawing the reins slightly, balancing on his thighs, rising in the stirrups.

It may have been the mare's heritage to know and to interpret those signs. She also gathered herself together, holding herself balanced as she followed the guidance of the reins, and she was ready.

Man and mare worked the beast out to the face of the camp. They put it through the last fringe of cattle, out on the dust-strewn open, and for a flash of a second the bullock hesitated. With a quick little patter of racing hooves, Amathea forced him out. Like a hawk Splinter swept in between the bullock and the mob, and that beast trotted over to the cut.

They put out six more cattle which ran quietly, the only trouble—if trouble it could be called—was in threading them through the camp to the face.

The last bullock there, a raking red and roan beast, had a dash of cunning allied to a strain of wildness. He had purposely been left till last, not to disturb the camp unduly. Kilgour sighted him, rode towards him.

Harry, riding past Terry, whispered quietly: "Give

'em plenty of room, Terry. I know that beast. Don't you go to come in too quick. Let th' boss take it right out himself."

Gradually man and mare forced the beast through the camp and had it on the fringe of the face. There the bullock hesitated, swung to the right, snapped about and was racing in the opposite direction in an effort to lose himself again in the heart of the camp.

Blend of the blood of begetters of incomparable stock-horses was matched against that bullock. The beast had taken but three strides and a half, shooting like a bullet from the gun, when a red lick of chestnut flame ranged up beside him. Amathea had seen the move coming. With her animal senses reading the bullock's mind, she was prepared for it. In her youth and inexperience, though, she bungled her start slightly, losing ground. Once set on the job, she had drawn on the racing beast with the ease of a hawk striking a dawdling finch.

The bullock thundered along the face, boring in, lifting clouds of dust, head down, tail flying. Beside him, lying up on him, shouldering him and forcing her weight on him in an effort to turn him out, was the maiden mare Amathea on her first camp! She was playing with the bit, flirting her head slightly, grimly determined, apparently enjoying herself hugely.

In a spurt of dust, a short-cut gasp, a momentary sliding of hooves and a raking of horns, in the snap of an eyeflick, the bullock turned and raced in the opposite direction, boring in and striving as desperately as before to regain the mob.

Kilgour's Mare

The bullock was racing confidently, knowing he had shaken off the man and horse which worried him. He doubled himself to turn in and gain the safety of the mob. But before the turn the chestnut flame ranged up beside him again, leant over him, forced him out.

The bullock took it in long runs, right along the full face of the camp. That was to the mare's advantage. She could hold him cheaply for pace. She enjoyed racing him. She revelled in the sport of it.

He tired, rolled his eyes towards the cut standing about a hundred yards distant, stuttered in his stride, propped, turned and trotted over to them.

Amathea, her heart pounding, the full joy of life tingling her veins, breathing in sharp gusts, flirted her head. The wind rippled her mane. She turned to go into the camp for another one. Undoubtedly "this is the life!" expressed her feelings.

"Steady, the little mare," Kilgour soothed her.

"Take that mob away and steady 'em before you lets 'em go," Harry called to a couple of the men. "She's a good un," he continued to Kilgour, riding beside him and admiring the mare. Under his breath he added, including the man with the mare: "They're a pair of good uns."

"Yes," Kilgour replied casually. "She ain't a bad mare. She's got the makings in her, Harry."

Chapter 11

THE COMMITTEE OF THE ILADDA PICNIC CLUB MET. They decided to hold a one-day meeting at the usual time. The station work was too constant and too strenuous to devote more time to racing. A one-day meeting would give the men two days to recover. A two-day meeting meant that a week would be required for the men to get over it.

Harry was interested in the committee's deliberations.

"Holdin' a meetin'?" he asked.

"We are," Kilgour said. "One day only, Harry."

"Runnin' Amathea?"

"I don't know. You see, Harry, there's too much work to do. We're not paddocking this year. We'll send up half a dozen horses. We'll work 'em good and solid in the camp. They're not to be galloped, though. A week before the meeting we'll give short bursts as pipe-openers to clean their winds. They'll be strong enough. All they'll want will be clean wind. And they're only to have one start each. We can't knock our horses about too much with all the work ahead of them."

"Runnin' Amathea?" Harry repeated.

"What's your weight, Harry?"

"Ride ten-seven easy enough."

"Evans has challenged me to meet him in the Breeders' Plate. That's welterweight-for-age. For a four-year-old that's about ten-ten, I think. I'll look it up and find out. He's got a three-year-old, by Lapidist from Seething, that he fancies. He hinted I wasn't game to meet him with Amathea. What about it?"

"Of course I'll ride for you," Harry said quickly. "I don't like that Plate, though. It's too short for the mare: it's only five furlongs."

"Don't make any error," Kilgour demurred. "Five furlongs is one of the most difficult races there is. It's a tough race, Harry."

On 24 May the one-day meeting was held.

The men gathered there knew that in the next six or seven months they were to pass through the fires of hell, each twenty-four hours of every day stretching in an eternity of drudgery. But this was a break, a snatch of pleasure. For the moment they were intent on taking a deep draught of the fun of living.

The first item on the programme read: "Breeders' Plate, for district-bred horses, bred by members or stations on which the members are employed, welter-weight-for-age, distance five furlongs, for horses that have never won a race."

Amathea, strangely excited by the awakening of an hereditary instinct, looked about her in wonder at the many people and various strange sights.

When Harry mounted her in racing colours with a light saddle, sweat broke out on her shoulders. It was only when she swung into the straight and thundered down between the lanes of people in her preliminary that she seemed to grasp the full meaning of the whole thing.

Then her heart pounded in great thumps, and she knew. The desire of her breeding woke in her. Good as it might be to cut out a rogue bullock, it was infinitely better to measure her paces with her peers. That was the insistent demand of her breeding.

The field lined up at the start. It being the first race of the day, and the only meeting of the year, the jockeys were a little excited. The horses, all maidens that they were, were some trouble to handle.

At last, to a wildly-waved flag and a stentorian "Go!" from the starter, a spurted cloud of dust proclaimed to the spectators that the race had begun.

Lapthing bounded out in front, scampering along the track like a harried hare, doubling himself together and stretching out with almost the action of a fox-terrier dog.

It was entertaining; it was attractive; it was, in its way, even pretty. But it was not galloping.

He drew away from the field, the others in hot pursuit. At the turn, where the angles made it confusing to judge distances accurately, he seemed to lead the others by at least six lengths.

Evans, with his quiet voice and staid manner, murmured behind Kilgour: "I thought those Lapidists were the best-bred horses about the district, Kilgour. I knew it was a mistake to send those mares to Bluff Downs. When they meet on equal terms, and without the aid of handicapping, they show their superiority, as I told you."

The field turned into the straight. Lapthing was still prominent.

Then a chestnut, a thing with a clean-cut, crooked stripe on its face, began drawing on the racing leader. The chestnut stretched confidently, picked itself up cleanly. Skimming low, it swept on Lapthing. It reached him, gathered him in a stride, left him, and, alone and hard held, took the lead.

"Amathea!" was the cry. "Amathea! Come on, Amie! Amathea on her own! Come on, Amie!"

Kilgour did not hear the clerk of the scales announce that the weight was right, neither did he hear the judge declare Amathea the winner of the Breeders' Plate. There was a curious lump in his throat which forbade speech.

He took his mare away, leading her about until she was cool, and Woppida was condemned to eternal damnation for the slowness with which he obeyed the many orders given him.

Kilgour stayed with his mare, crooning to her, taking her muzzle in the crook of his arm and laying his cheek on hers while he swore at her affectionately. He sat on a log and admired her, finding pleasure in the way the mare looked about her and in the red flare of her funnelled nostrils.

He was disturbed from his reverie by Harry, in jockey's costume, coming towards him.

"Hulloa, Harry!" he called. "I haven't shouted for you yet. Come on and we'll go and have one. What's all the row about?" he asked as a sudden cheer burst on them.

"That's th' declaration of th' Templeton Handicap," Harry explained. "Mr. Hopkins won it with Changwagee. We run fourth with Destinous."

"Has the Templeton been run?" Kilgour demanded in surprise. "I wanted to have a bit of a bet on that. I was thinking of other things. This dry time's got me going. I can't help worrying about it. Never mind. We'll go and have a drink now. You stay here, lookout belong-it that one mare, Woppida. I'll skin you alive if you go away and leave her."

The races finished, the men returned to the stations, and the drudgery of endless work continued. Scarcely had the fats been delivered and the last of the sale cattle started on the road when waterholes required attention. Those which usually lasted till October and November commenced to dry about the end of June.

Cattle running there had to be shifted to other waters, distributed to avoid congestion, and pumping plants on the bores commenced to work. That was a further worry to the management, and it necessitated endless work for the stockmen and horses.

Kilgour used the car more frequently to get from place to place more quickly, supervising work and seeing that all was as well as was humanly possible. But his two riding horses, Amathea and Cherry, received their full quota of work. Each of those mares knew what it was to pace through the long night, their hoof-beats sounding singularly sharp and clear in the night air, and to be let go at the home yards little before daybreak.

"It's all part of your graduation course, Amie," the man told his mount. "You've got to stand up to it, mare. It ain't much fun for either of us. It's the endless monotony of the thing that takes its toll, even though you do seem to go more freely at night than in the daytime—the same as nearly every other horse. You passed the first big test when you whipped that Lapthing affair at the races. One more test, whatever it's going to be, and you're fully qualified. And I don't pass you, me lady, until you do qualify!"

With summer's heat coming early in October cattle had to be handled in a hurry, and handled carefully. Waters went away with appalling rapidity. Almost, it seemed, the scorching sun burnt the nutriment out of the grass.

Then a new danger arose. From away in the southeast a black pall hung in the sky, and at night that horizon was lit with a red glimmer of distant flames.

A fire, starting about Boulia somewhere, swept up the western side of the river. Its right wing followed the course of the channels, unable to cross that bare-eaten strip. Its left wing was away over in No Man's Land somewhere, three or four hundred miles out in the Territory.

"We can't do anything," Kilgour remarked to Harry. "We haven't the man power in the district to handle it. We must have a starting-point, a base, and we ain't got that with a fire that size. Anyway, we might as well puff against thunder with a kitchen bellows as try and cope with that thing. It's out of our class. We'll take a ride over to-morrow—you going down the river and me up it—and we'll see what's happened."

On the morrow, riding Amathea, Kilgour went across the river. The fire, with the whimsical fate which seems to control all bush fires, had burned erratically. For no apparent reason it had left untouched and unscorched patches of a thousand acres or more. But in the main, the western side was swept bare and presented a black scar on the face of the earth.

Kilgour rode up to the face of the fire. It was burning easily, hissing and crackling. Its shroud of smoke was pierced by sweeping hawks. They used the flames as beaters. They knew by instinct that the flames would hunt quail and other ground-running birds from the protection of the thick grass. When these bewildered atoms rose from the flames the hawks took a turn.

When the leaping fires reached a patch of rotting

cane-grass in a low-lying swamp, and with a rush the flames leapt in the air, crackling and roaring, Amathea wheeled in terror and tried to break away. In less than half an hour she was stepping unconcernedly through low flames, taking no notice of them, obeying the guidance of the rein and thigh of her rider as equably as if the fire did not exist.

The cattle were shifted across the river and put on new waters and feed. It was a job fairly big in its magnitude to gather about eight thousand cattle on horses which had to be handled carefully, but it did not require meticulous care: any few stragglers left behind could eke out a living on the patches the fire god had spared. Still, it was a work which took its toll of the horses.

Early in December, when summer's hot breath swept like a blast from the furnace, storms gathered. One played on the western side, lightning ripping and thunder rolling. From that western side, when eddying puffs of wind swung from it, there came the heavy smell, sweet of wet earth and rain.

"Go across and have a look what happened, Harry," Kilgour ordered next morning. "Take Paddy with you and send him up the top end to see what's on up there. I'm afraid it ain't much. It was like two bulls sparring: all bellow and dust, I think. Have a look and let me know."

Next night Harry made his report: "Nothin' doin'. Might 'a' been twenty points all told. Nothin' any good nowhere. That storm dragged a lot of cattle back over that side. There's fifteen hun'red or more waterin' at Brolga."

Kilgour surprised his head stockman by asking: "Are you any good at prayers, Harry?"

"Never tried much," Harry admitted.

"Then give it a flick. You might be good."

Chapter 12

THE CATTLE WERE SHIFTED OUT AFTER FEED AND water. Then, less than a week later, the storms started. Lightning ripped across the sky in streaks of flame, while thunder rumbled and rocked the air.

The rain pelted in driving waves; gradually water commenced to collect. Pads and gullies started to trickle; they fed creeks and streams which flowed into the river, then that mighty monster came with a rush. Laughing deep down in his throat, carrying froth on his breast and foam in his teeth, he swelled and burst his banks.

Almost overnight, it seemed, the ground clothed itself anew in green, and, bursting with life, the earth responded to the full season.

Birds chirruped and sang, going about the business of life which called to them. Flies, mosquitoes and sandflies sought what they might devour. Frogs with pulsating throats vibrated the night air and throbbed a clamorous bedlam from every swamp.

The stock themselves, responding as the earth did, seemed almost as if they too had been lying fallow in waiting for the rain. They fattened and grew almost while a man looked at them. They played and waged sham wars, bucked and skipped in the joy of life and the pleasure of living.

About the middle of March Harry took a ride down the bottom end. He wanted to note how the cattle were running, and to make his preparations for the first branding muster.

Returning to the station that afternoon, riding the chestnut mare Cissie, he opened the gate into Mingeri, deciding to go through that paddock and have a look at the stallion and mares. He found them out on the Turkey Plain, clustered together and swishing their tails to combat the flies.

Tooley Street came out of his mob. He pawed the earth and raked the ground, and as the man rode round the group the stallion also swept about them, keeping between the ridden horse and the brood. He held his head low, his ears lopped and the whites of his eyes showing.

"You're a bit above y'self, me joker," Harry commented. "Th' feed's a bit too rich for you. It's lyin' crossways in you. Get back, there! Keep back, I say, or I'll cut you in slices!"

The stallion was uneasy. He swung on his hind heels, reared, struck at nothing and squealed, lowered his head and sniffed the ground. Then, bursting into a flame of fury, he launched himself straight at the man and the ridden mare.

Harry swung his mount slightly. His whip struck the horse full across the outstretched face. The stallion ignored it. He may not even have felt it. He chopped with his gleaming fangs at the man's thigh, missed, and, as the whip smacked again, reared and struck with his hooves.

One hoof took the man about the shoulder, sliding down his arm, tearing his shirt and leaving strips of skin and flesh dangling. The other landed behind the saddle, quivering the mare as the shock took her. As the man swung his whip handle, taking it as a light cudgel to fight for his life, the stallion swung and lashed with hind hooves.

Cissie was cowed. She swung, in spite of the man's attempts to control her. In panic, she tried to flee. She had not gone twenty yards when the stallion flashed before her, wheeled her, reared and shook her.

Harry balanced the steel-lined handle of his whip, measured his distance, brought the knobby end of the handle down with a crash between the stallion's eyes.

Tooley Street released the mare. He shook his head to clear his dazed senses and turned to trot back to his mares.

Harry meant to push the moral home. He swung his whip again; it bit the horse's rump, left a red weal on his loins.

As the whip bit him Tooley Street wheeled.

Harry fought for his life. In that desperate onslaught of flashing hooves and gleaming teeth he sought to control his mount and combat the stallion. He barely felt injuries which should have rocked him. When his mare sank to the ground beneath him, wilting under the murderous attack, he only knew he was close to a tree. Without knowing what he did, he sprang, grasped a low limb, hauled himself to safety.

Tooley Street struck at the mare on the ground. He raked the body with the teeth, spun and lashed it. Then a movement from his brood attracted him. He charged at them, swung round them and held them in a bunched and trembling heap while he stood between them and the body on the ground.

It was well after dark before Harry, sore and cramped and tortured by ants, dared to descend from his perch. The mares had fed away, and Tooley Street had gone with them. But, though it was not in the direction of home, Harry followed a line of timber for a mile or more which took him to the boundary of Mingeri.

Thankfully he climbed through the fence. It was twelve miles to the station. He was sore, wounded, also he was unused to walking, and his light riding-boots were not fitted for the job. There was nothing else for it, however. He set his face for home and commenced to walk.

A little before three o'clock next morning Kilgour, dozing in his bed on the veranda, dreamt he heard dragging footsteps coming along the boards towards him. He thought he heard Harry Peelben calling him, and in his dream he wondered what Harry might want. Then a hand touched him, and Harry's real voice sounded close.

"Mr. Kilgour!"

Kilgour sprang from his bed and struck a match.

"Great, suffering—"

He checked himself as Mrs. Kilgour, carrying a lantern, appeared before them.

"Harry!" she gasped. "What happened?"

"I didn't mean to wake you, missus," Harry mumbled his apology. "I just come to tell th' boss he killed me little mare Cissie."

"Who, Harry?"

"Tooley Street—"

Kilgour caught him as he reeled. With the book-keeper Brinkworth helping, he carried Harry to a bed, stripped him and assisted while Mrs. Kilgour bathed and cleansed the wounds.

"There don't seem to be anything serious," he muttered. "How's it, Harry? Drink this sip of brandy. Are you hurt inside, old man? How are you—right?"

"I'm right," Harry mumbled. "I'm a bit knocked about, but I'm right."

"If you're crook, Harry, say so," Kilgour urged. "I'll get a doctor somehow."

"I'm right," Harry repeated. "I'll go to me bed now."

"You'll stay right here," Kilgour ordered.

Next day Kilgour started for Mingeri, riding Cherry.

After dealing with sundry station matters, he wrote to the firm.

I regret to report that the stallion Tooley Street was to-day found dead in Mingeri. He had a bullet in his forehead. Possibly this was done by some traveller or kangaroo-shooter, as Tooley Street has lately developed into a man-eater and is liable to charge at sight any one entering his paddock.

To Peter Outhwaite he wrote:

In my letter to Head Office to-day I stated that Tooley Street had been found dead in Mingeri, and I hinted that a traveller or a kangaroo-shooter had shot him. I shot him. I shot him deliberately. He savaged Harry Peelben, killed the mare Cissie, and nearly killed Harry. He has been hovering on the edge of developing into a man-eater for some time now. I think the flush of the season brought it to a head. I told Head Office that someone else had done it, as they might not care to think their manager rides about the run shooting valuable stock. I am telling you the truth, so you can break it gently to them. Of course, between you and me, if they want to get rid of me, I am prepared to go. I would do the same again, though. But if they do not want to get rid of me, as I hope they will not, then I have given them an excuse to cover me over the loss of the stallion.

Chapter 13

HARRY'S WOUNDS HEALED CLEANLY, LEAVING ONLY scars, memories and the sullen regret that, as Tooley Street was dead, it left him no chance for retribution.

The mail brought letters from Peter Outhwaite and Head Office.

Outhwaite's remarks, in reference to Tooley Street, read:

I'm sorry you had to shoot him, George. Serve the cow right. I'd like to have seen the fight Harry put up. Congratulate him for me, will you? I told the firm the truth about the horse's death, and I explained your attitude to them. I think they are writing you this mail.

The letter from Head Office, after dealing with sundry station matters and acknowledging receipt of various reports, added:

We note with regret that the stallion Tooley Street is dead. If, as you say, he was developing into a man-eater, perhaps it is the best thing that could have happened before he did serious harm. You will require a new stallion on Meetucka, and in this connexion we would appreciate your advice.

"I missed my vocation, Nell," Kilgour remarked to his wife. "I should have been in the diplomatic service."

The time came round for the annual races. With a good season assured, the price of stock reasonably right, and with their sporting instincts responding to the period of fallow, in which they had been lying dormant, managers and men gathered in great heart.

Alby Baldwin was there, grinning expansively, and his glinting spectacles flashing welcome to all. Colin Dale, neat and dapper, hard of face and soft of voice, and with the instincts of a gentleman. Long Bill Raven, happy and prepared at any time anywhere to argue on any subject, employing sonorous words of many syllables. Angus Carran, with a smile of welcome and a cheery invitation to old friends. And others—many others. And, of course, the ladies. From many miles—hundreds of miles—they had gathered in strong force. The omens were good.

Lapthing won the Breeders' Plate, the opening race of the first day.

"That just goes to prove what I said," Evans contended: "The Lapidists are the best-bred horses in the district."

"Why didn't you do it last year?" Kilgour demanded.

"I was racing at an unfair advantage last year," Evans replied, apparently almost believing himself by the sincerity of his voice. "Your mare, that just beat him, was a four-year-old. Lapthing was only three."

"But you insisted previously that weight-for-age equalled those matters."

"Weight-for-age is not framed for western grassfed conditions," Evans replied unctuously. "You had an advantage last year."

"And how about the three-year-olds your fellow just beat?" Kilgour asked triumphantly. "How about them!"

"The conditions are different this year, Kilgour. We've had a good season. It makes all the difference."

Tom Hopkins beckoned to Kilgour, and he joined him.

"Did you hear the whisper?" Tom asked.

"What?"

"They say that Peeramon's a ringer. He's Blatique, a disqualified horse from inside. Ted Bolton, head stockman from Merrima, got a loan of him from Ginger Forbes. He worked Ginger in as Joe Forsyth so's to get him to ride the horse in The Bracelet. Ginger's a disqualified jockey, too. Blatique's a horse with big performances inside, and he's nominated him here as a maiden. What about it?"

"That's the worst of a gentleman's club," Kilgour spat irritably. "A man expects 'em to act as gentlemen. It's beyond 'em, it seems. I wonder if Evans is in this.

He was terrible keen to make side bets with me that Amathea wouldn't win The Bracelet. I want to win that race for the wife, too. My mare, on account of her win last year, carries ten-ten. That joker, who should be giving her weight, gets in as a maiden. I'm not starting the mare to-day, as I don't want to get more weight put on her by winning—I want to win that Bracelet particularly. They're not starting Peeramon to-day; saving him for the betting in The Bracelet to-morrow, I suppose. This is going to be interesting, Tom."

"Let's disqualify the cows."

"We can't, Tom. We accepted Peeramon's nomination. We gave Joe Forsyth a permit to ride. Now the onus of proof is on us. If we'd taken action before accepting the nomination, then the onus of proof would have been on them—that's the way I look at it. I don't know if it's racing law. It seems to me to be an equitable thing, though. If we can prove anything, we can dump 'em. If we only go on rumours, then they dump us."

"Let's go and have a drink," Hopkins suggested. "This puts a dirty taste in my mouth. Blast 'em!"

"And now," Kilgour added, as they turned from the bar at the booth, "let's go and have a look at Peeramon."

"We can go and have a look at the Merrima string— they're down there in the trees," said Hopkins. "But Peeramon ain't with 'em! What do you think of that?"

They walked down to the Merrima horses. Peeramon was not among the half-dozen or more tied to trees. Bill Blackstone, Joe Forsyth's mate, clean-shaven, suave, neatly dressed, with his tongue under perfect control, met them.

"Where's Peeramon?" Hopkins asked, in his bluff way coming straight to the point.

"We didn't bring him to the course to-day, Mr. Hopkins," Bill answered politely. "He's a very nervous horse, and we didn't want to upset him."

"How do you know he's nervous?" Kilgour demanded. "How do you know he'd fret on the course?"

"That's Ted Bolton's idea, Mr. Kilgour," Bill said. "Ted is an expert horseman. He understands them."

"If he's a maiden, as his nomination says, and if Bolton only got him four months back, how does he know what he's like on a track?" Kilgour asked.

"Really, I haven't any idea," was Bill's even response. "I never saw either Bolton or Peeramon before I came here. I was out of a job. Joe Forsyth told me Ted would give me a job looking after the horses. That's how I came to be here. If there's anything I can do for you I'd willingly help."

"Euchred!" Hopkins blurted in disgust, turning away and walking back to the course. "It's no good to us, George. We can't twist and dodge the way those fellows can. We've got to run straight. But the minute that bloke wins a race we get him examined by the police; we take his photo and his full description. Do you think the little mare can wheel him?"

"I'll be the proudest man in Australia to-morrow if Blatique's the horse I think he is, and if Amathea does wheel him," said Kilgour.

The first day's races drew to a close. The night was

made hilarious by the loud laughter of glad men, by the popping of many corks, by the jingle of silver and rustle of paper money. Music and singing sounded from various quarters. In the hall feet shuffled over the floor, dancing in time to the groaning wail of an accordion.

Next day, after early lunch at the pub, cars, horses, men on foot, sundry blacks and odd dogs raised the dust as they trailed to the course.

The postmaster, who was closing his office for the afternoon, hurried across and gave Kilgour a telegram. He read it casually, read it again more carefully, re-folded it and put it in his pocket. Then, as Mrs. Kilgour and her party got in the car, he drove to the course.

Several horses were objects of interest. Amathea held her own court, and obviously she appreciated it. But as the rumour had spread, Peeramon was the centre of attraction. All the members of the committee individually drifted by him, stopped and looked at him. As Kilgour and Hopkins arrived Joe Forsyth was in attendance.

"Amateur rider! Him!" Hopkins snorted. "A man can tell he's been reared in a stable by the way he rubs the horse down, and I never seen a disqualified jockey that didn't slip a saddle off a horse like that. Him! Amateur! P'ff!"

Three races were run. Then the secretary rang his bell and announced "Weigh out for The Bracelet."

"I'll bet on th' field," the bookmakers took up their battle-cry. "Even money th' field. Two to one bar one.

I'll lay! I'll lay! I'll lay! Two to one bar one. I'll bet on th' field."

Gradually, as the money came in, the odds righted themselves: "Even money Peeramon. Three to one Amathea. Five to one Dotson an' Cheerful Flat. I'll bet on th' field. Even money Peeramon an' eight to one Lapthing. I'll lay! I'll lay!"

"There's fourteen horses in the race, and Peeramon's at even money!" Hopkins whispered to Kilgour. "That's not a funny price for a maiden, is it? He brought twenty quid in the Calcutta too! We'll watch this bloke, George."

"If he's what his people think he is, we won't need to watch him," Kilgour replied. "He'll force himself on our attention. What chance has Changwagee, Tom?"

"I wouldn't like the missus to know, as she has hopes of wearing that bracelet; but he hasn't got a dog's chance," Hopkins replied calmly. "It's between your mare and this ringer, George."

Peeramon, an upstanding bay with a white face, aged, showing plenty of breeding, swung his head and looked about him as he entered the straight and turned for his preliminary. He came stretching past the men who were watching him intently, sweeping along with the trained action of an educated horse.

"Amateur rider or disqualified jockey, which?" Hopkins grunted, elbowing Kilgour and drawing his attention to Joe Forsyth's seat and hands on the horse.

"H'm-m-m!" Kilgour murmured. "That boy's been well schooled, to say the least of it."

Amathea swung at the entrance of the straight. She bowed her chin in on her chest, held hard on the bit, and her tail streamed behind her as she stretched to the gallop. She skimmed low, belly-to-earth, perfect mistress of herself, and apparently in command of both time and distance. Powerfully yet daintily she revelled in the action and enjoyed the pipe-opener.

As the field collected at the milepost, manoeuvring for position, Evans joined Kilgour and Hopkins as they watched the start.

"I'll bet you an even tenner that Peeramon beats Amathea, Kilgour," Evans suggested tauntingly.

"Done!" Kilgour snapped, his pride in his mare touched. "Amie's at threes, Peeramon's even money. It's not a fair bet, but I'll take you. You mark that bet, Tom; one to get a place—"

"They're off!" Hopkins shouted, adding his voice to the chorus which supplied that gratuitous information.

The field thundered past the stand, throwing up the dust. In a packed bunch they charged the first turn.

Going down the side they strung out considerably, and a straggling tail had begun to form. Lapthing, whose mission it obviously was to set the pace, scampered along in front, leading by lengths, with Dotson in hot pursuit. Eelman, Dunstan and Ratskip were prominent. Datron, out of the hunt and hopelessly beaten, laboured behind.

In the pack, lying in behind the leaders, were Amathea and Peeramon.

They raced along the back, individual horses hard to pick at that distance and through the dust.

Lapthing fell back beaten, Dotson took his place for less than a furlong, and he, having reached his limit, was swallowed in the pack and hidden.

They turned and came up the side. In that thinned field half a dozen horses could be picked who had a possible chance. Changwagee was in the ruck labouring to hold his place. He, with others, dropped back as the real horses sorted themselves out to fight the finish.

The crowd was getting restless, calling first one name and then another, and bookmakers, ever eager to help, offered odds to each name as it was called.

As they swung round the turn for home all the colours flashed into clear view for a second. Then, as the field settled in the run for the post, and the spectators could note without error what were the positions, one great shout went up:

"Peeramon!"

Racing strongly in front, laid up on the rails in a good position, and with his rider sitting firm and motionless, Peeramon held a commanding lead as they raced for home.

"The bet is as good as won," Evans said quietly.

Even as Evans was congratulating himself, and while the crowd was reconciling itself to a tame finish, the chestnut flashed from the field. Head outstretched, tail streaming, foot by foot and yard by yard she crept on the leader. Half-way down the straight she was at his girths, and behind them thundered a beaten field.

"Amathea!" was the cry. "Come on, Amie! Amathea! Peeramon! Amie! Come on, Peeramon!"

The mare crept up, measuring her opponent stride for stride and gaining an inch at a time. She drew up to his shoulders, to his neck, and, as they came towards the grandstand, she was on even terms with him. They were locked together, splendid specimens of a superb breed, with courage unsurpassed and determination of incredible quality. Neither flinched, and the yells of the crowd in hysteria urged them to further efforts. Peeramon drew away slightly, gaining less than a head and holding his position.

A sudden silence fell. They, who a moment before had been shouting madly, held their breaths. The thin voice of a child shrilled, sounding as sharp as breaking glass after the volume which had preceded it.

Kilgour, all the love and pride of his mare welling up in him, was standing beside the rails, gripping one, his knuckle joints showing white under the intensity of his hold.

"Stick to him, Amie!" he muttered. "Hang to him, girl! Stick to him, mare! You can beat him! Stick to him!"

Amathea came at her opponent again. She drew up with him, grim, determined, implacable, inflexible in her will to win. Coming to the winning-post, the lead alternated between them. Both horses were running true, straight, picking themselves up cleanly and stretching to their work, giving all they had to offer.

Harry was riding desperately. He was a perfect horseman. But compared to the finished artistry of the trained jockey beside him, Harry's efforts seemed rough, unpolished, crude. In the paddock, after cattle, or on the plains, there was no comparison between the two men as horsemen. There on the racecourse, riding a race, again there was no comparison between them— one was a trained specialist, the other a bush product.

Slowly, almost imperceptibly, Peeramon drew ahead, and Kilgour was tortured as he watched. His mare came again in bulldog tenacity—and then, that for which he watched, waited, and almost prayed, showed itself. In the flash of a stutter Peeramon's front legs spread slightly, and Forsyth felt for his whip.

"Now, Harry! Now!" Kilgour shouted in a tumultuous explosion. "Now, Harry! She's got him! Great God, she's got him! Got him!"

The horses were only ten yards from the post, less than two full strides, and Peeramon's tail twitched ominously. He floundered as he cracked under the strain exerted by the relentless thing that pushed him, and before his jockey could snap him together again that chestnut which would not acknowledge defeat swept on him.

As they flashed past the post one full-throated roar broke from the crowd as hats were tossed in the air and men danced in their excitement.

"Amathea!"

The clerk of the course, drunk with the excitement of the stirring finish, galloped wildly after the field to return with the winner, while the spectators, finding relaxation in ridicule, cheered him satirically.

The clerk returned leading Amathea. He made his

way through the lane of people who flowed to the right and to the left to give him a passage.

The mare was palpably on edge, her eyes protruding, her nostrils distended. She walked with a springy action, which showed she was on her tiptoes of excitement. But she held herself under control, and the influence of the pale-faced, gasping rider on her back restrained her.

As Kilgour went to meet his mare, his face grim, his lips trembling and showing a dead-white line, he dared not do more than flash a look of gratitude to Harry. As he walked beside her a whisper or two sounded on each side of him; a small splutter of cheers broke out from behind him. Then, as Harry slipped off at the scales, there came ringing cheers from those bushmen—those horsemen and horse-lovers—who had momentarily been stunned to silence by the excellence of a performance rarely their luck to witness.

When the excitement had simmered down a little, which was after several toasts had been drunk, after Mrs. Kilgour had surreptitiously lifted her veil to powder her nose, showing eyes red-rimmed, and after Kilgour's hand tingled from repeated handshakes, he and Hopkins drew apart a little to talk rationally.

"She's a great mare, George!"
"She's a great mare, Tom!"
"She's a beauty, George!"
"She's a gem, Tom!"
"Will you sell that mare, Mr. Kilgour?" Black-

stone asked, appearing suddenly. "I'll give you fifty quid for her."

"Go to hell!" Hopkins snapped.

"Take him away, Tom," Kilgour pleaded. "Take him away where I can't hear him. If he makes me a good offer I can't, in justice to my owners, refuse it. Take him away."

"I'll give you sixty," Blackstone continued, when Hopkins's leg-o'-mutton fist fell on his shoulder, twisting him and turning him away.

"Will I kill him, George?" Hopkins asked cheerfully.

"Not to-day, thanks, Tom," Kilgour replied. "Take him away somewhere."

"Come with me over behind the booth," Hopkins addressed his captive. "There's a quiet place there where I can cut your ears off."

Kilgour drew the telegram from his pocket, opened it and read again:

Following your advice have purchased The Diver for Meetucka.—Outhwaite.

Chapter 14

OF THE VARIOUS SOCIAL EVENTS WHICH STIRRED THE district during the year there was only one of real importance. There might, and would, be several dances, sundry Cinderellas and various other diversions. But the Iladda Picnic Club's Ball stood alone. It was the only function of the year for which, and at which, the ladies wore evening dress and the men laced themselves in the regulation harness of dinner suits and dress clothes. For an hour or more, perhaps, the men looked unhappy and self-conscious in that strange garb. The ladies, on the contrary, blossomed like night-blooming flowers. For that one night of the year they enjoyed themselves to the full.

The ball was held at Mungalo station homestead. The extensive lounge was made gay with streamers of bunting and with ropes of flowers culled from several station gardens. At one end of the lounge, on a temporary dais, the many silver trophies, the prizes of the meeting, made a brave display, throwing strange lights as dancing shadows fell on them and passed.

Kilgour was preoccupied, inattentive and absent-minded. He was obviously worried about something. For an hour or more he twitched uneasily. Then he drew off one white glove, and with a pencil devoted himself to the back of his programme. He drew parallel lines and crossed them at intervals with others running at right angles. He divided those oblongs, starting from the top and duplicating each as he went a step farther down, and then on that miniature pedigree form he wrote names. He found satisfaction in that occupation until only the top space of all was left blank. He frowned at it, tapped his pencil on the seat beside him, trying to recall a name.

Tom Hopkins, catching Kilgour's eye, jerked his thumb over his shoulder and grimaced a wink almost loud enough to hear.

"What's up, Tom?" Kilgour asked.

"Come away," Hopkins suggested. "Us old fools are out of our place here. Come with me, George. I've found out where they keep the bar."

"There ain't any bar," Kilgour corrected him. "I got called to order over the same thing about half an hour ago. There's a bar at the pub and a refreshment booth at the course. But here at the ball, Tom, we don't have common stuff like that: ours is a buffet. We'll go and have a look at it."

"And behind it," Hopkins continued eagerly, "there's a little room with three or four chairs in it—a thing that's just made for fellows like you and me."

"It sounds good," Kilgour admitted. "Lead me to it."

Their drinks secured, Hopkins toasted:

"Here's to the future!"

"Here's to to-day!" Kilgour replied. "May I never forget it!"

They had just settled themselves in their chairs when Evans entered, standing in front of them.

"The Peeramon fellows want to race you in three months' time under other and more equal conditions," he informed Kilgour. "They're willing to put up a side bet of a level hundred pounds."

"Can't be done," Kilgour grunted. "A hundred's too much for me."

"You won more than that to-day, surely?" Evans hinted.

"When I get your tenner I'll have a bit more than it," Kilgour said. "Anyway, the mare ain't going to race again. She's going to the stud."

"What!" Evans gasped. "Going to the stud! Why, she's just in her prime."

"Which is the reason she's going," said Kilgour. "That gives her a chance to hand on her perfections to her progeny. She ain't any wasted frame, and she's not a half-formed child. She goes at her top, with the ability to hand on her virtues. Anyway, who frames these equal conditions they want?"

"They are to be left to me," Evans said. "What about it?"

"You've got my reply," said Kilgour, chuckling at the absurdity of the suggestion.

Evans, in response to a call from outside, left.

"That fellow," Kilgour remarked, "wants to be handicapper, starter, judge and steward of the match, leaving me only to fill the part of the mug. You'd hardly think a full-grown man could be so silly."

"How about washing the flavour of it away?" Hopkins suggested.

Settled again in their chairs, the two men recounted the events of the meeting, and to their hearts' content they talked horse.

"You told Evans you were putting Amathea to the stud," Hopkins said. "What horse are you sending her to?"

"Have a look at this, Tom." Kilgour pulled the telegram from his pocket. "What about that?"

"What's this Diver?"

"He's a horse I fancied. I wired Peter Outhwaite to get him if possible. Wait a bit. Just hang on a second till I get his pedigree from out of this inside pocket. There you are! What about that!"

"H'm-m-m," Hopkins agreed, wriggling in his chair. "I say, George, I don't think Providence gave a man a neck just so's he might have something to wrap a stiff collar round. Do you?"

"Ease it, Tom. It ain't glued on, is it? Now, we

must have a sire strong in Stockwell blood to return to those Bluff Downs mares, particularly Amathea. The Diver's a tail male descendant of Stockwell through the Melton line. Besides that, he's got the modern lines of Cyllene and Kenilworth—a horse noticeably strong in Stockwell and tracing to Pocahontas herself."

"I'd like a dash of Musket," Hopkins argued. "Think of old Carbine, George; of Wallace, Trenton, Martini-Henry, Pistol; a score of others."

"It's good blood, Tom. It's real good stuff. But I don't fancy it too strong for station horses. The Muskets are inclined to throw too high behind and pitch too low in front. We've got it here in this pedigree, sufficiently diluted to make it attractive. We get it through Kennaquhair's dam Calluna, by Manton, a good un, and a son of Musket himself. I say, Tom, do you think Providence gave a man feet so's he could put 'em in patent-leather shoes?"

"Are they pinching, George?"

"Like hell, Tom."

"So're mine. We'll take 'em off."

"How about having a look at that boo-fay affair, Tom? We don't want it to escape while we ain't looking."

"To the future," said Hopkins.

"To to-day," Kilgour replied.

"Now, let's have a look at that pedigree again," Hopkins asked, returning to his chair and lowering himself carefully: "He's by Rivoli. I seen that fellow, George. We were in Melbourne and seen him run in the Cup. You talk about a race! That bay fellow was giving Bitalli, the winner, twenty-nine pounds. And he made him run a record to beat him, too! He's a horse, George, very near perfect, and with shoulders on him that a man wouldn't think were real if he didn't see 'em in the flesh. If The Diver's like his sire he'll do me!"

"Then we get shoulders through his dam," Kilgour put in. "She's by Kennaquhair, by Kenilworth. That Kenilworth was perhaps the best-shouldered horse we ever had in the country. Some of his stock might have been a bit high for station horses. But he's right. Kennaquhair was a big fellow, on the leg a bit; but he won the Sydney Cup, beating that living marvel Poitrel. All that Kenilworth stuff stays, and stays well, with whips of stamina and tons of guts."

"He ought to be a great horse," Hopkins agreed. "Do you think Providence would let a man be born naked if he was intended to wear a coat, George?"

"Mine cramps my style, too," Kilgour agreed. "Let's take 'em off, Tom, and hang 'em on nails. Got a smoke on you?"

"Divil a smoke," Hopkins replied. "The missus reckoned it was vulgar for a man to suck a pipe in these clothes. We'll have to chew cigarettes. Jack's got plenty in that boo-fay. I'll call him to bring us some."

"We'll go and get 'em," said Kilgour. "Jack might be lonely, looking after that boo-fay by himself. Anyway, it's up to us to hold the thing in its place in case the others want it."

THE DIVER 1

RIVOLI 5

REPARTEE 5

MELTON 8

MASTER KILDARE 3
- LORD RONALD 7
- SILK 3

VIOLET MELROSE
- SCOTTISH CHIEF 12
- VIOLET 8

BACK CHAT

ST. SERF 8
- ST. SIMON 11
- FERONIA 8

CHAT MOSS
- MACHEATH 13
- CHATELAINE 5

LADY BABBIE

NEIL GOW 1

MARCO 3
- BARCALDINE 23
- NOVITIATE 3

CHELANDRY
- GOLDFINCH 4
- ILLUMINATA 1

THRUMS

SYMINGTON 20
- AYRSHIRE 8
- SYPHONIA 20

ROSEMOUNT
- ORVIETO 1
- ROSE BOWER 5

PEARL ROPE

KENNAQUHAIR 2

KENILWORTH 3

CHILDWICK 19
- ST. SIMON 11
- PLAISANTERIE 19

KIZIL KOURGAN
- OMNIUM 2nd 22
- KASBAH 3

CALLUNA

MANTON
- MUSKET 3
- TRES DEUCE

HEATHER
- GOLDSBROUGH 13
- RECUEROO 2

REAL PEARL

SYCE 1

CYLLENE 9
- BONA VISTA 4
- ARCADIA 9

SKYSCRAPER
- AYRSHIRE 8
- CHELANDRY 1

YOSEMITE

HAUT BRION I
- ST. SIMON 11
- BONNIE LASSIE 1

MERIDIAN
- MARDEN 2
- SUNSTROKE 1

"Well, here's to the future," Hopkins proposed a minute later.

"To the memory of to-day," Kilgour pledged.

"Let's have a look at that pedigree again," said Hopkins.

Chapter 15

THE YEAR DREW TO A CLOSE, ANOTHER SEASON CAME and went.

Late in June, riding the bay mare Destiny, Kilgour left the head station for a day's inspection, going through Mingeri.

The day was cool, with a touch of ice in the mid-winter air. For a brief spell the eternal south-easterly held its breath while the giant behind it gathered himself together for a longer and more sustained blow. The sun, shining with the white intensity peculiar to that clear atmosphere, struck glinting rays from dancing leaves of trees, and from every swaying blade of grass twinkling lights shot and winked. The air was clean, dry, brittle, snapping with sparkling life, vital.

Kilgour rose in the stirrups, drew deep down in his lungs a plenitude of the life-giving air, and settled in the saddle while the mare swung along, pricking her ears, tossing her head and playing with the bit.

Ahead of him a cheeky willie-wagtail chirruped as it flew in its jerky flight, snapping minute insects and coming back to the horse to get anything which its moving legs might brush from the grass. Over on the left, on the bare claypan flat, a flock of corellas many thousands strong covered the earth as with a blanket of snow. As the man rode closer the corellas nearer him rose in the air, hovered above the flock feeding on the ground, and settled on the far flank.

Almost from beneath the mare's hooves a little ground-lark rose on palpitating wings. It fluttered for a second in the air, hesitating whether to rise higher or to return to the sanctuary in the grass. With a hissing swoop and a clear "Tap!" of talons striking, a black falcon took its breakfast on the wing.

Kilgour dismounted and opened the gate into Mingeri. He rode across the paddock, alert for signs of horses or for recent tracks of them, and, when crossing Turkey Plain, over on the edge of timber on the other side of it he saw the stallion and his mares. They were grouped together, standing in little bunches, swishing tails to hunt flies which were non-existent at that time of the year. Odd pairs stood a hundred yards distant from the main mob.

Colleen saw the man first. She never lifted her head, moved or made a sound. She merely pricked her ears and concentrated her attention. Immediately every member of the group swung to attention and faced the ridden horse coming to them.

The Diver came out of the mob, his chestnut coat ablaze with flashing fire as the sun shone on it. He stood out clear to defend his brood. He raked the ground, lowered his head and snorted, and, after calling his clarion challenge, trotted out to meet the horse from which the man had just dismounted.

He was a magnificent specimen of a thoroughbred, and Kilgour admired him as he came. He stood fifteen-two or a shade under it, low-set and with great depth of girth. His barrel was sprung like a cask, with square back ribs, great strength of loins and with depth of quarter. He reared and played as he came nearer, showing to advantage his superb length of rein and shoulder. He advanced his nostrils to those of the mare the man was riding. Then he turned and went back to his mares. His curiosity was satisfied, his fears of a rival were groundless, and his advances had been repulsed. But he stood watchful and alert, between his brood and the man who rode about them.

Cherry, with her chestnut colt hugging her close and rubbing against her chest, pricked her ears and lifted her head as Kilgour called her a greeting.

The first drop of The Diver's foals were interesting. Though Kilgour admired them as they deserved to be admired, and though he commented on them and drew on his imagination for the enthusiastic praise with which he lauded their mothers, he was not satisfied. He rode about the mob a second time, rising in his stirrups to see that no unit escaped his attention.

Amathea was not there!

Then he saw her. In his eagerness he had overlooked a patch of mimosa growing near the bank of a gully. Partly hidden behind that he saw a tail swinging, and dimly he caught the outlines of a horse. Blurred though those outlines were, made indistinct by shadows and by intervening foliage, he knew his mare when he saw her.

Amathea was standing, her head hanging low, immediately over a dark outline stretched on the ground. As the man approached her she swung to face him, her head up, her ears pricked, her eyes shining. She turned and dipped her head quickly, merely brushing the smudge on the ground with her lips. As though touched by a switch, it jerked to its feet and stood.

It was a chestnut, with the same markings as its mother. Its stubby little mane was twisted in tight crinkles, and its wisp of a tail was water-waved in crisp curves. It stood at its mother's chest, looking out from under her neck; and, though poised for flight, every aspect of that little thing's bearing bespoke defiance. Its head was held high, its eyes bright and glowing, and it shuffled its pinhead hooves in its anxiety for action. Then, borrowing assurance from its mother, it turned casually and went to her flank to drink.

"You gem!" Kilgour exploded. "You priceless little gem! Take care of it, Amie!" He was thinking: "I don't suppose I'll ever ride and work that thing as I did you. But I'm going to have a heap of fun watching it grow. I suppose, if you were a story-book mare, you'd come to me when I called you, and you'd bow your neck and rub against me in your pleasure while I handled your foal. But you ain't a story-book thing,

Amie—you're real. If I dismounted you'd fly on the wings of the wind, with that long-legged little brat speeding beside you like a dancing shadow. If I did catch the foal, and if I tried to handle it, you'd come at me like an Amazon bereft, and you'd tear me to pieces if you could. You're natural, Amie. I think I prefer you that way, too."

"You're home sooner than I expected, George," his wife greeted him. "You're just in time for afternoon-tea. Come and have some."

"In a minute, Nell," he replied. "I've got some work to do in the office that can't be delayed."

"Can't you have your tea first?" Mrs. Kilgour protested.

"Very well," he agreed. "But there's one thing, Nell—a very short un—that won't take long."

In his office Kilgour pulled out a drawer, and from the back of it, from under some papers, he took a rolled sheet. He had hidden it there months previously, pretending to himself, as it was out of sight, that he had not done it.

He unrolled it, showing a fully tabulated pedigree of the united breedings of Amathea and The Diver.

He drew the sheet to him and smoothed it. He dipped his pen in the ink, and in the blank space left at the top, which was to show the result of the union of Amathea and The Diver, he wrote in capital letters:

"EVARNE."